Cosmic Love:
A love that spans the cosmos.
A reunion of two souls on the physical plane.
An embodiment of the universe's most powerful energy.
A love that heals past, present, and future wounds.
A love that heals Mother Earth.

Testimonials

"When I think of magic, I think of Sierra. One day she simply asked me what I wanted, and I replied with, "I think I'm ready to meet somebody. The one." She responded with, "Well, let's chant for him. Tell me (and the Universe) what that looks like for you." It was through this guided chant and meditation with Sierra that allowed me to powerfully manifest the love of my life .... within 32 minutes of chanting for him! What made this even more powerful was that Sierra was there to witness this magic unfold! Thanks to Sierra, I am a practicing Buddhist and still madly in love with my cosmic love partner! This ever-so powerful book will share all of Sierra's secrets to have you manifesting the love of YOUR lifetime."

Dr. Shabnam Islam

"How To Attract Your Cosmic Love Partner" is so effortlessly informative and valuable. The tone is friendly and the themes easy to comprehend and digest. The homework is fun and some of the exercises I had been meaning to so a years, but just needed that push. I loved hearing the success story of Sierra's love life, as living proof that these concepts actually work – it's not all just in theory. She is a walking example of what happens when you put in the work, and I'm SO excited to continue this journey with her now as my love coach. I even have an amazing man in my life now that I am starting to date, which I attribute to doing the work in this book!"

Kelly Pantaleoni, Actress, Humanitarian, Writer & Producer

"The Cosmic Love Guidebook provides an awakening experience that changes the way you approach dating. I felt as if I was dating in the dark. Not sure what I was looking for, or why I liked someone. After noticing a series of unsure relationships, a friend introduced me to, The Cosmic Love Guidebook which helped shine light on how to identify what is important to me in a relationship and provided a guide to stop blindly dating. After reading it, it gave me the tools to date with a purpose and with a clearer understanding of who would be the best partner for me. This book changed my life and helped guide me to find the person of my life, my wife."

Demetrius Freeman, Photojournalist

"*Sierra is a mystical conductor on the love train, ensuring all who hop aboard will arrive to their cosmic love destination as well as enjoy the ride along the way. Sierra is an ambassador of true love reminding you to never settle on what you truly desire and to believe that you will receive what you ask for while preparing you along the way. She has laid out in this book exactly what she has practiced in her own life journey manifesting her dream partner and helped me do the same. I went from being as single as a pringle, to blissfully married to my dream man, with the guiding hand of Sierra's support and love. If you are ready to believe in cosmic love and receive your deepest desires manifested in your dream partner, this is the book for you!*"

Tiffani Marie Wilshire, Divine Communicator

"*Sierra's book provides great wisdom and exercises for everyone. As I read it, I could hear Sierra's voice giving me hope, confidence, and encouragement. I had just started seeing someone, but I completed each activity carefully and still find myself revisiting my workbook to remind myself of what I want and deserve in a partner. In previous relationships, I found myself letting things slide and accommodating my partner. Sierra's writing reminds me to stay true to myself and let my own light shine as brightly as possible. I know her book helped my love bloom. I've never felt more confident in a relationship, and I am so grateful.*"

Jessica Alberi, The Conscious Classroom Teacher

SPRINGBOARD EDITION

Sierra Sophia Mercier

How To
Attract Your Cosmic Love Partner

A Guided Workbook

© 2023 Author: Sierra Sophia Mercier
Published by: © 2023 Springboard Edition

ISBN Print: 978-3-96496-015-3
ISBN Ebook: 978-3-96496-016-0

Springboard Edition
Ulrike Posselt, Strasse des Friedens 17, 07381 Poessneck, Germany
Printed in different locations worldwide.
https://springboardedition.com

How To Attract Your Cosmic Love Partner Guided Workbook

The lessons in this book contain guided exercises and opportunities to journal, so have a pen or pencil handy. Writing down our goals, dreams, and desires has been proven to help us attain them.

Introduction

*"You and I, it's as though we have been taught to kiss in heaven
and sent down to Earth together,
to see if we know what we were taught."*
Boris Pasternak, Doctor Zhivago

The night I fell in love, as in knew I found, "The One," was one of the most significant moments of my life. It was New Year's Eve. My boyfriend at the time, Andre, and I had only been dating for one month. We met after I found his ad online seeking a roommate. I answered the ad, came to see the place, we hit it off, and the next thing I knew he offered me his extra room; two weeks later I moved in. There was physical tension and clear attraction between us right away, and I had told myself that if he didn't make a move in two months, I would make a move, GASP! Well neither of us had to wait that long because he kissed me on the second night. So, we were living together right from the start, which is rather unconventional. I mention it because it gives context to how we knew so quickly that we wanted to spend the rest of lives together.

Back to New Year's Eve, 2011. We were at a rave in San Diego, losing ourselves in the thick of the dance floor, and just before midnight, Andre whispered into my ear, "Sierra, I don't know how I could ever leave you." I turned and kissed him. Then he whispered again, "Sierra, I love you." I smiled as if I was being seen for the first time and said in return, "I love you too." The rest of the evening we were floating on a cloud of love. Our merging of energies literally created a forcefield around us. It was as if an explosion of love erupted on the dance floor, a "lovesplosion" as we affectionately call it.

The following day is when my life really shifted. I found myself crying, no, sobbing uncontrollably for 8 hours straight. It was as if a dam broke, and lifetimes of stifled tears all came rushing at once. They were simultaneously tears of joy, and tears of sorrow that had no rational reasoning behind them, other than a phrase that pulsed beneath the surface, "I found you, again."

With this statement as my mantra, I felt like I could see our souls out in the cosmos reuniting in this lifetime. The weight of it felt like we had lived many lifetimes apart from each other. The more I fell into the womb of, "I found you, again," the more the tears just kept flowing and cleansing my spirit. Without hesitation, Andre just held me the entire time, no questions asked. It was as if he knew there was a great healing moving through me.

I didn't tell Andre about this feeling of finding him, again. But then later that evening, Andre had his own emotional release and when I asked him why he was crying he said, "I just can't believe I found you again."

This is what I call Cosmic Love, and I know that each and every one of us has our very own Cosmic Love Partner out there looking for us, yearning for us. I compiled all the steps I took, and the realizations I had that enabled me to manifest this kind of relationship and put them into this step-by-step guided workbook. My wish is for you to start making your way toward your Cosmic Love Partner too.

I believe The Beatles were right when they sang, "All you need is love," and that this force we call 'love,' be it romantic or otherwise, is our north star as individuals and collectively. If we can all start moving toward our north star of love, we will make our way home, back to harmony and balance with all that is. Imagine a world where everyone is living in and with love. Can you picture it? Close your eyes, and just pause for a moment to visualize the abundance we could co-create with love as our foundation. Know that the steps you take within this workbook are leading you, and leading us all to that place, and for that I say, thank you!

"If the spirit of many in body but one in mind prevails among the people, they will achieve all their goals, whereas if one in body but different in mind, they can achieve nothing remarkable."
Nichiren Daishonin

Preface

Someone once asked me, "What makes your book different from all the rest?" What she was also saying was, "I've read all the other books about bringing in "The One" why should I trust you? What could you possibly say that will help me when all the other ones haven't?"

What I believe sets my book apart, is the greater mission we are on behind the quest for love. I am a firm believer in connecting our personal desires to something greater than ourselves. I believe this supercharges our intentions and goals. It is well and great that you want to find true love, or have cosmic love in your life, but then what? In this book, I am inviting you to call on love for the sake of humanity, for the sake of transforming the dark in the world into light. The work in this book is guiding you to do just that. By connecting what's in your heart to the greater purpose of the universe, you will magnify your power, increase your chances of meeting "The One," and you quite possibly might manifest something even beyond your wildest dreams.

There's really only one way to find out if this book will be different for you than all of the others. My hope is that you give it a shot. Risk going on a bad date. Risk not having good chemistry with someone. Risking making a mistake, or an awkward hookup. This book will either inspire you or irritate you, but whatever it does, just know that I have such deep faith in love as a healing energy, that if you commit to the work in this book, at the very least, you will walk away touched and transformed.

Acknowledgments

Thank you to Uli for seeing the potential for this book from the beginning, for your support and guidance to get it to this place, and for believing in my mission of Love.

Thank you to my parents for bringing me into this world, for loving me unconditionally and supporting all my big adventures. I love you for infinity.

Thank you to my husband, Andre, who has been my greatest teacher in the school of Love. You have enabled me to float and fly when I was scared to even leave the ground. You are my favorite everything ever.

Thank *you*, my friend. Thank you for allowing me to be your Cosmic Love guide. Thank you for putting your trust in me to be the voice of love that lives within you already. You have been called to this book because you are ready to receive the type of love that spans the cosmos; an unbreakable, firmly grounded, yet totally expansive kind of love. With the assistance of this workbook, you are about to embark on a transformational journey, and I am so happy to be the one you have chosen to pilot this spaceship of love. I am with you every step of the way, so don't hesitate to reach out for guidance should you need it.

"A great human revolution in just a single individual will help achieve a change in the destiny of a nation and, further, can even enable a change in the destiny of all humankind."
Daisaku Ikeda

Welcome to your Cosmic Love Partner Workbook!

You are your own best compass, so as you make your way through these exercises and lessons, take what feels right for you, discard what doesn't, or come back to things at a later date if you wish. Life isn't linear, so do what *feels* good in the moment because that is your inner compass guiding you.

My own love story starts with a journey of overcoming sexual and emotional abuse at the hands of my figure skating coach for over four years. Through embarking on an inner self-transformation journey, I was able to turn my experience of "poison" into "medicine," and ultimately attract the most incredible life partner and love into my life. I transformed from being someone who attracted men who didn't value me, who used and abused me physically, sexually, and emotionally, to attracting a life partner who loves me beyond the reaches of the universe. Truly a cosmic kind of love. I know that I'm not alone in this type of story. Many women share this experience of abuse. I share my experience as an offering so that it may potentially help you in your journey to finding and attracting your Cosmic Love Partner.

You don't have to have experienced abuse to get something out of this book. If you are totally over attracting duds, or relationships that just aren't working out, or you are feeling like maybe you will never meet "the one," but you still really want to find true love, then this book is for you.

Get ready to work! I chose to structure this as a workbook because manifesting requires taking action. This guided workbook is divided into five steps: helping you move from doubt to faith; helping you create your list; helping you get clear in mind, body, and spirit; helping you transform your inner landscape so that you can attract the best partner; and then finally a collection of my love lessons to help you find and keep true love flowing.

This workbook is meant to guide you, and comfort you as you seek authentic, loving relationships in your life. I have written this book from the perspective of Buddhist philosophy, but if that's not your spirituality of choice, that's OK. It can all be translated through the filter of your heart.

The tone and guidance of this book are aimed particularly at encouraging women. But men have also benefited from this guidebook!

I believe that when women stand up and shine their intrinsic light, it will cause men to have to do the same. The more light you can cultivate within your own life, the more light you will attract in a deserving partner.

STEP 1

DOUBT VS. FAITH

"Trust resides squarely between faith and doubt."
Warren G. Bennis

STEP 1: Doubt Vs. Faith

This is the launching pad into the atmosphere of Cosmic Love. Before you can even begin to manifest your Cosmic Love Partner, we must address the elephant in the room: Doubt.

Doubts and Fears are born of the same energy, so to counteract them, we will also explore the worlds of Faith and Trust. If the word "faith" is sticky for you, like it was for me for many years, insert: "belief."

"The single word 'belief' is the sharp sword with which one confronts and overcomes fundamental darkness or ignorance."
Nichiren Daishonin

Everyone has doubts. Doubts are normal and necessary for our growth. Without them we would be machines. Doubts make us human and elicits emotions, for better or for worse. But even stronger than all your doubts, is your faith! The power you possess to believe in possibility, to believe in the unseen aspects of reality, this is your lifeline to attracting cosmic love.

So, before we takeoff, let us address and transform anything holding you back from believing that true, cosmic love really does exist for you.

Doubt

Calling out and naming things is an important step in transcending. I will name some common doubts; highlight whatever resonates with you, and feel free to add your own:

"True love doesn't exist."
"Everyone abandons me."
"What if I never meet the right person?"
"What if I'm not meant to ever get married, or find true love?"
"What if I'm not meant to have children?"
"What if they're not the right person for me?"
"What if I meet someone else?"
"What if *they* meet someone else?"
"I'm too old, no one will want to marry me."
"I'm too old to start a family."
"All the good ones are taken."
"Everyone I meet is a dud."
"Something must be wrong with me."
"Love is a hopeless quest."

_____

_____

_____

_____

_____

_____

_____

Doubts and insecurities are completely normal. Especially in this buffet culture of online dating, it's as if the options are endless, which creates a "grass is always greener" syndrome and a false sense of "there could always be someone else, someone better." In addition to that, with online dating people are judging each other based on the tiniest fraction of who they are, and the pressure is off from having to make a real heart to heart connection. There are seemingly endless reasons to abhor the dating scene, and there are endless doubts to be swept away by. You could literally spend a lifetime doubting everything and never run out of doubts. But please don't do that!

In my experience, doubts and fears are sneaky and come in all shapes and sizes too. "Am I too pretty for them?" "Are they too good looking for me?" "What if I could do better?" "What if no one will ever love me?" These questions we have seem like small, annoying thoughts that bring us down from time to time, but over time they build up and begin to create the very thing we are trying to avoid. The more energy we give to our doubts and fears, the more we will experience opportunities that validate them.

My relationship with Andre moved at lightning speed. We met through a roommate ad online my second day in Los Angeles. Two weeks later we were living together, as roommates of course, but we both knew there was something firing that felt spicy. Our chemistry was mutually electric and a week after living together he asked me, quite romantically, to be his girlfriend. Three weeks later, on New Year's Eve, we fell in love and knew we would spend the rest of our lives together. In February he asked my dad for my hand in marriage. In March we were designing an engagement ring together. September, he proposed. Let me tell you, this was not my plan!

I moved to Los Angeles with the intention of being what I called, an "acting monk." I wanted to focus solely on my craft and career of acting, and my spiritual practice. In my first career, I was a competitive figure skater. I trained with the best skaters in the world. I was training to *be* one of the best skaters in the world, and I knew what it took to be the best – laser focused dedication. So, new to LA, I told myself I didn't want to date, at least not casually, I just wanted to do "me." But now here I was, caught up in this meteoric vortex of the greatest love I had ever experienced. A love that cracked me wide open, shifted paradigms, healed lifetimes of heartache; a love that ultimately led me to writing a book about love! This wasn't your typical love and suddenly I found myself engaged to be married less than a year after arriving in LA. Not to mention the fact that the trajectory of our love vortex was only getting started.

I wanted to try and slow things down by having a long engagement, so we set our wedding date for a year and a half out. "Haha!" said the universe. After our engagement, I signed up on TheKnot.com for all things wedding related. Shortly thereafter, they announced a sweepstakes for one lucky couple to win the first ever, "Knot Dream Wedding," an all-expenses paid dream wedding experience on Valentine's Day.

Five months after Andre asked me to marry him, we found ourselves the winners of this Dream Wedding grand prize, walking down the aisle in Bryant Park, New York City in a worldwide streamed wedding to say, "I do!" I even had the fortune of giving an ice-skating performance at our wedding. (You can watch the whole experience on YouTube if you want.) Needless to say, we felt like the universe was orchestrating our (re)union to happen sooner rather than later.

The problem was, I am the quintessential free spirit who dances through life to the beat of her own self-composed symphony. This high-speed love train of "'til death do us part" began to scare me. Quiet, insidious doubts emerged from the depths of my mind making me question, "What have I done?" "Did I do the right thing?" "Is this really what I want for the rest of my life?" "Am I making a mistake?" "What if...this, what if...that" scenarios ping-ponged in my mind causing spiritual distress. Like a graceful swan though, I never outwardly displayed my doubts, nor did I share them. I kept them to myself while pressing forward with a smile.

It was at my hometown wedding reception where an intuitive family friend tapped into my doubts and called me out on them. She was visibly distraught and told me the ancestors were so upset. She didn't have to say any more than that and I knew exactly what she was talking about. In that moment I realized that all my fears and doubts about my husband and our marriage were writing code into the ether leading us toward pain and misery.

If our thoughts help write, create, and paint our future, then I was starting to paint a very dark picture. As soon as I could, in my next chanting meditation session, I deeply apologized to our ancestors and spirit guides, and I vowed to never take Andre for granted again. I prayed to heal my doubts and fears, and to honor and cherish Andre for the gift that he is.

When I realized what I was inadvertently creating with my doubts, it was as if I was given a glimpse into my future. I saw pain, sadness, darkness, and illness. So, I set about to rewire my doubts with appreciation and gratitude, trust, and faith, and most of all, *love*. All things this book helps you to cultivate. It took me years of continual examination and choosing of love, but it was well worth it. My life and our love blossomed in ways I never could have imagined, and it continues to do so until this day.

But what if you don't have a psychic friend to tell you that you are upsetting the ancestors? Or, how do you know if your fears are founded or not?

In my experience, fears are shaky, they are not solid and sturdy, and they usually live in the easily swayed mind. Love on the other hand, is a fortress; it is grounded and lives in the center of the body. Fear vibrates at a very low frequency and therefore triggers us to make poor, often regrettable, emotion-based causes (actions). On the contrary, love vibrates at the highest frequency and arouses wisdom, courage, compassion, inspiring us to make more healing causes (actions) for our life.

This is where stillness of the mind, self-reflection and meditation come in to assist you. Get in tune with the wisdom of your body through movement like ecstatic dance. Listen to your heart through journaling and spending time in nature. Experiment with plant medicines if you feel called to explore that world. These are all practices that have helped me and can also help to bring you soul-level clarity. More on clarity in **STEP 3: Finding Clarity**.

The next time you are feeling doubts of any kind come in, pause for a moment. Close your eyes and check in with your body. See if you can set your fears and doubts aside for a moment and ask what your higher-self, your love-self really feels, knows, and believes to be true about your situation.

Your mind is like a radio. The thoughts you are spending time thinking are the frequencies you are projecting and the channel that gets picked up and received. Doubts and fears keep us small; they keep us stuck, and they prevent us from tuning into the very thing we are longing for: love! When we think and act from a place of love, we will never be steered wrong. When we think and act from a place of integrity, truth, and faith, then even if things fall apart or challenge us, we will have the wisdom and confidence to know that it is part of our growth and necessary shedding. When we begin to tune our mind to the channel of "faith" (insert "trust" or "belief"), we open the doors leading us toward our Cosmic Love Partner.

Two weeks after Andre and I first met, the intuitive friend I spoke about earlier told me that she had a vision of Andre and his family on the other side of this ornate golden door with white light shining from behind it, and I was at the opposite end of this hallway lined with all these open doors. She said that if I wanted to go through the last door, I had to close all the others. I knew what she meant because I had a tendency to keep doors open, keeping everyone as friends and as potential future options. Now I was faced with finding the faith to go against what felt safe to me.

I trusted her vision and guidance, and I followed through with closing the open doors. Acting on this faith rewarded me exponentially. Faith, although it can be scary at times, pulls us out of the quicksand of doubt. It sets us on a course of possibility. Faith, trust, belief, whatever you choose to call it, opens the door to our greatest self and our grandest love.

"Doubt is a pain too lonely to know that faith is his twin brother."
Khalil Gibran

Faith

Faith is a must-have component on the quest for cosmic love. Faith is also testing. The word alone used to send shivers down my spine. I was someone who rejected religion, considered myself an atheist, and the word "faith" *really* bothered me. It took me ten years of Buddhist practice to become comfortable with the word "faith." This says to me that we can overcome anything. We can transform our most negative biases into something that can actually serve us.

Cosmic Love requires faith. It requires believing that your person is out there looking for you too. It requires believing that you are worthy of the greatest love of all time. And even when you have found said love, faith is required for keeping that love going.

It may seem that the longer you are searching for love, the harder it is to maintain faith that love is possible for you. Those pesky doubts arise working overtime to make you feel unlovable and unworthy. Trust that these are precisely the grounds upon which you are meant to transform your karma. Trust that these are the exact training grounds you need to unearth your greatest confidence, your most deeply valued self, and the most cosmic of love!

If having this kind of faith is something you struggle with, you are not alone. The number one thing women fear most with relationships is abandonment; falling so hard and then not having it work out. The love that is possible between you and your Cosmic Love Partner is worth facing that fear head on. Do not hold yourself back from love in fear of being hurt. Heartbreak happens to all of us, and you will get through it. If it doesn't work out with someone you deeply loved trust that there is an even greater love waiting for you. Speaking on behalf of women here, I believe this fear stems from the deep root of not truly valuing ourselves.

In Buddhism we have a concept called, "Voluntarily assuming the appropriate karma." It means that we sign up to go through various struggles and challenges, and by overcoming them, we are then able to help and encourage others going through the same struggles. This is also known as the Bodhisattva path.

It is my belief that when a soul chooses to incarnate as a female, they are signing up to go through the challenge (karma) of having a disbelief in the value of their life. We are talking about tackling thousands of years of programming that "men are superior to women." Some scientists believe patriarchy has roots spanning as deep as over 2 million years! As women it is coded into our DNA. Inside that extra X chromosome is the belief that we are somehow inferior, less-than, or not equal to men, which leaves us in today's modern dating world still waiting to be chosen, and still believing that if no one loves us, something must be wrong with us. It is only recently in the last hundred or so years that women have really begun to raise their voices and stand up against this notion. We still have a long way to go, but **you** deciding to awaken to your true value, **you** deciding to see yourself as a container for infinite love, **you** realizing how precious and valuable and incredible you are helps to rewrite that code for yourself and future generations. It also helps to bring men back into harmony with their feminine, and ultimately it will help move the collective needle toward a more peaceful society and world.

So, thank you for taking on this mission of generational transformation! Thank you for waking up to your worth. Shining your newfound light through the power of love is going to illuminate the darkness shrouding our world. This is a huge undertaking, but the fact that you are here, in this lifetime, reading this book means that deep down you believe that you are meant to help us all be in more harmony and peace. Peace thrives in love. We are the microcosms in our own minds and hearts, in our relationships and families, for that worldwide love and for world peace.

EXERCISE: HUG TIME!

Find a nice quiet, comfortable space, close your eyes and hug yourself. Wrap your arms around your body and really feel yourself. Feel the body you have been given. Now send love to that body and say, "Thank you body for holding me, housing me all these years, I love you body!" And next say, "I love you (insert your name here)! You are so full of love, you are so brave and courageous, you are so beautiful, worthy, valuable..." Say whatever feels good to you in the moment, and even if you don't quite believe everything you are saying right now, continuing a practice like this will transform you. Imagine that with each "hug time" exercise, you are recoding the cells in your DNA to reflect the type of love you want to call in and receive from your Cosmic Love Partner, your CLP for short.

STEP 2

MAKE YOUR LIST

"You create your thoughts,
your thoughts create your intentions,
and your intentions create your reality."
Wayne Dyer

STEP 2: Make Your List

In 2008 I made a list of all the things I wanted in the "perfect" partner. My heart had just been broken, and in an attempt to leave a possibility for this person to come back into my life (leaving a door open), I made my list based off of them, but then I embellished it. At the time, certain things felt important to me, but over time as I matured, many things became less important. Three years later when I met Andre and pulled my list back out, it was seriously uncanny how many things he matched, including some very specific physical traits.

Andre and have been together since 2011, and believe it or not, my love for him only continues to deepen and grow. I'm in love with his face, with his spirit, with his tattoos, with his sensitivity, with his skills, everything. Even the things I have had to learn to love over time because no one is perfect.

There was one night in particular, Andre and I were lying in bed, looking into each other's eyes, speaking loudly in silence. As I lay there face to face with him, transfixed in the depth of his gaze, I felt the power of my list, simple scribbles on a piece of paper, come together in physical form right before me. Why did I write what I wrote? Why were some of those things so important to me, even if over time they became less so? It's as if there was an unspoken knowing living within me whispering to me as I wrote my list. Which makes me wonder...

What if the aspects that we personally find important for a partner to possess: physical, emotional, spiritual, and beyond, are actually deep soul memories encoded in our DNA working to draw us back to our CLP?

If that leaves you with more questions than answers, allow me to explain: Each one of us has a very different idea of what is important to us in a partner. These differences are like the differences in our fingerprints. I believe they come from past life memories or agreements, ancient wisdom like cellularly coded guideposts helping to lead us toward "the one." "The one" can be interchanged with Cosmic Love Partner, or twin flame. For some, a soulmate may fall into this category. More on these differences later.

We have the power to give everything in our lives meaning. Everything can be a sign. Everything has purpose and value if we let it. So as you prepare to write your list, center yourself, get present, and listen to the whispers great and small that come up from deep within. Don't judge them too harshly, don't brush things off as silly. Those things you find important in a CLP, might just be part of the treasure map leading you back to one another.

If you want to find the best partner for you, they need to possess certain qualities that are important to you. In order to even begin calling that person in, you must have a written list of those important qualities and non-negotiables. Feel free to get as creative as possible with your list and be specific. Don't forget to have fun with it too!

The universe loves specificity. If you walked into a restaurant and ordered a sandwich, there are literally hundreds of different types of sandwiches that could be prepared for you, and they may serve you something you don't like. If you ordered a sandwich with romaine lettuce, heirloom tomato, extra avocado, sprouts, cucumber, veganaise, dijon mustard, and pickles on gluten-free bread (yes, I live in L.A.) then you are going to get the delicious and specific sandwich you ordered. Don't be shy about being specific in order to get what you want.

I will also share some options for how to create a ceremony with your list. You can be like me and just stash your list somewhere, or you can try out some different rituals and ceremonies with your list. If I went back in time, I would "ceremonialize" it. Personally, I love ceremonies. They are physical representations of intentions, and intention setting is powerful, magical stuff.

In the next section, we are going to make your detailed MANifest or WOMANifest list, followed by my optional ceremonies to seal the deal. Disclaimer: I am not trying to exclude any gender identities here. This is simply a play on words. I am fully supportive of people choosing to identify themselves in any way that resonates with them. LOVE is LOVE.

In the following section I have broken things down into categories and provided some examples just to get your juices flowing. Feel free to use them if they resonate for you or cross them out and come up with your own unique ingredients. Use the empty space below for your musings.

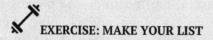 **EXERCISE: MAKE YOUR LIST**

Character Traits

Examples:
Is truthful and honest
Is caring
Is kind to me, and others, and their family
Is generous
Has a good and similar sense of humor
Loves kids, is great with kids, and wants to have kids
Is self-motivated

Lifestyle

Examples:
Is spiritual or open to spirituality
Loves to travel
Loves camping and the outdoors
Doesn't smoke or drink excessively, etc.
Is plant based or veg-curious

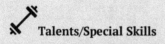 **Talents/Special Skills**

Examples:
Is great with computers
Loves snow sports
Is handy around the house
Enjoys cooking

 **Physical Appearance**

Examples:
Doesn't have back hair (or maybe you don't care)
Is taller than 5'8" (if that's important to you)
Is athletic
Is Italian, or part Asian, etc.

All Others

Examples:
Feels like fireworks when we kiss
Loves and gets along with my family
Is worldly
Is well educated
Is happy in life
Has a job they really enjoy

Voila, celebrate! Your list is crafted, and now you are ready to start preparing to meet the potential candidates.

When I made my list, I was only 22. My heart was broken by someone who was in my life only for a short amount of time, but he made a deep imprint on me. I took all the aspects I loved about him and magnified them, while adding more specific things as well, until my list included 80 or so different ideals for the "perfect" partner.

Yes, you read that right, 80. I wasn't kidding around! A lot of these things became less important to me over time, but I still kept the list tucked away in a journal, in a drawer, in a nightstand. In essence, I sort of forgot about it and went on with my life. One and done.

Around this same time, I was introduced to Nichiren Buddhism and began a daily spiritual practice. I mention this only because of what it did for my life. My daily Buddhist practice, consisting of chanting *Nam-myoho-renge-kyo* and studying Buddhist principles, started transforming within me what I consider to be a vital key to attracting true love: *developing self-worth*.

Whether you choose to chant, meditate, pray, spend time in nature, or perhaps all of the above, if done so *consistently* and *sincerely*, you cannot help but begin to feel a deeper sense of value emerge from the depths of your life.

It took time of course, but after just a few years of consistently self-reflecting, and naturally bringing out the best in myself, a process in Nichiren Buddhism called "human revolution," I noticed that my confidence, self-worth, and a deeper understanding of my inherent value began to bloom. I went from being someone who often let men determine my value, to someone who realized how truly valuable I am. In response, I came to believe that the man I was going to marry one day would be the luckiest man in the world. Not from an egoic place of "I'm amazing and must be worshipped," but from a place of finally understanding how much I had to offer as a human being with infinite love to *give*.

✗ EXERCISE: LIST CEREMONIES (optional)

The following suggestions are not based in any fact or documented custom; they are just different ways to set your intentions into motion.

Feng Shui suggests keeping your list under the bed. After you have completed your list, place it under your mattress, and allow the universe to do the rest.

A woman I once knew told me she was instructed to take her list and go outside on the next full moon, find the Big Dipper constellation, and intentionally place each item on her list into the Big Dipper. Then wait and see what happens. She manifested her dream life partner who checked off everything on her list this way. However, one thing she left out was, "doesn't smoke cigarettes." Though this was important to her, she didn't think of it, and her dream guy ended up being a smoker. This didn't stop her from being with him though. She made the determination to help him quit smoking, which he did! Last I heard they were happily married. Specificity is crucial.

Create your own! Find your own way to seal the deal with your list. Get creative and make it special. Maybe you place it on an altar for meditation, maybe you paint the words into a bowl, maybe you go to the beach or a lake and pick up a stone, set each item intentionally into the stone and throw it into the water. Have fun and just go for it.

STEP 3

BE THE ONE
TO RECEIVE THE ONE

"True and lasting solution to correct ills can be found only by inner, collective transformation of human beings."
Nirmala Srivastava

STEP 3: Be The One To Receive The One

Oftentimes in relationships we are seeking for someone to fill a role in our lives. We think that if we find that perfect person, all of our problems will vanish, and we will live happily ever after. It's not our fault. Unfortunately, we have been spoon-fed this myth since we were children, and we continue to buy into the same story when we see everyone's picture-perfect lives online. The truth is, it's not until we look inward and fulfill our own quest for happiness that we can really be ready to receive that ideal partner.

My CLP appeared after I took some very concrete actions in my life. They are as follows:

1. I started working on my inner landscape and did my human revolution; I changed from within.
2. I followed my dreams. I did me; I listened to and pursued the intelligence of my heart.
3. I was clear on what I wanted, yet open enough to receiving whatever the universe had in store for me.

This next step is going to help you get started on taking your own clear actions toward becoming "the one" that you wish to receive.

Changing Poison Into Medicine

When I was 16, I left home and moved to an international training center with all the hope and determination in the world to one day achieve my goal of becoming an Olympic figure skater. My parents helped me relocate so I could train with the best skaters and coaches from all over the world. Within less than a year of training in this new environment, I was reaching new heights competitively which led me to believe that I was on the right track.

Shortly after I turned 17, my coach, who I had built a strong bond of trust and friendship with, crossed the line and sexually abused and assaulted me. The power dynamic was confusing, because not only was he nearly 10 years older than me, but he was also an authority figure telling me what to do on a daily basis. Over time he made me feel special and "chosen," and our relationship as coach and student began to blur into something much muddier. This confusing and unhealthy relationship went on for over four years. It involved secrets, deceit, lies, infidelity, and abuse. He had groomed me into his personal sex object, all while I was trying to train to compete at the elite level. Sadly, this is not uncommon in the world of figure skating, or sports for that matter. When young women are coached or influenced by adult men, abuse often happens behind closed doors.

The hardest thing for me to accept was that this destructive relationship with my coach ultimately prevented me from reaching my figure skating goals. Our blurred relationship held me back and caused my dreams to slip away. Of course, I didn't see it like that in the midst of things. Once I moved away to another state, and began a spiritual practice, I was able to reflect on my past. I learned to meditate on things in a deeper way. To look within and ask myself, "Why did this happen? What was this trying to teach me? What can I learn from this?" I realized that it was my karma to attract men that didn't respect me, and that abused me in one form or another. I also realized that deep down, it was an effect of not truly valuing myself. I could finally see from a higher perspective that I had given my value and worth away at the expense of my biggest dreams. I will admit, this was a hard pill to swallow.

Once I saw things through this awakened lens, I was able to begin the process of transforming my karma from someone who allowed themselves to be used and abused by men, into making the determination to never let myself be treated less than I deserve. I began to see myself as an infinitely valuable being, and I decided that I was not going to settle for being treated as anything less. In Buddhism we call this process, "Changing poison into medicine." There is no experience in life that we can't transform into something of supreme value. No matter what trials and tribulations we encounter, we have the power to transform them into our greatest benefits.

After making this new determination, and establishing a daily practice of cultivating deeper self-worth, within three years' time, I completely revolutionized who I was. I became my own cheerleader with encouraging self-talk as opposed to negative self-talk. I believed wholeheartedly in my inherent value as a woman. I became more loving, open, friendly, and confident. All these elements added up to finally opening the doors that brought a man into my life who could mirror it all back to me. When we change, our environment changes.

When struggles occur in our lives, we have two choices. We either allow that challenge to defeat us, become bitter, angry, resentful and feel like a victim. Or we allow it to propel us to greater heights, learn something about ourselves, and grow from the experience. You are the script writer of your life, and you are the star. At any moment, you can write yourself a new scene and lead yourself toward a new destiny. You can actively transform an event that appears negative (poison), into an outcome that benefits you (medicine). Oftentimes all it takes is a shift in perspective and a little faith. The rest of this book is aimed at helping guide you to a place of higher perspective.

Self-Worth

Self-worth is one of life's great lessons for each and every one of us. I deeply believe that cultivating healthy self-worth is the activation key to attracting your CLP. In this day and age, (I'm looking at you, social media) self-worth needs to be a daily discipline; it's our life's job, and it's an essential component to attracting the best partner.

When I was younger, I had no concept of self-worth. No one taught it to me. I thought I had to do things I didn't want to do for men to like me. I sacrificed my own needs, desires, and even integrity to be "loved." In short, I allowed myself to be treated less than I deserved. A couple years after starting a consistent spiritual practice, a greater sense of self-worth just naturally began to grow within me. I realized that I am a treasure of the universe. I realized that I have an infinite amount of love to give and receive, and that whomever I ended up with was going to be the luckiest man alive. I know I said this before, but I'm saying it again because I want you to engrave it into your life.

What happened next? Did I meet Mr. Right? No, not right away. Each person that came along helped me learn how to deepen my self-worth even more. They each built upon the other and taught me what is important to me, and not important in a partner. I continued to hold firm in my newfound belief of my true value, and three years after making my list, I met my husband.

In hindsight, I realized that each person that came through my life was gifting me with another opportunity to deepen my sense of self-worth. One helped me respect my time and energy more. One challenged me on my values. But rather than waiting to learn these things in hindsight, try to look for the transformational opportunities in real time.

For example: Let's say you start dating someone, and they live a little far from you. They always want you to come to their place because they say their schedule doesn't allow them to come to you. Rather than always appeasing them, take a moment to reflect on if this is an opportunity for you to deepen your sense of self-worth and say no. *Your* time is valuable too. Ask that you alternate, and they come to you once and a while. If the other person can't honor this request, then they have shown they are not truly that into you.

My dad told me once that he hitchhiked across multiple states to go see my mom. He said, "True love will move mountains to be with someone."

Self-worth is about honoring the treasure that you are. When you begin to value the treasure of your heart, and practice self-respect, you will begin attracting individuals who value and respect you back.

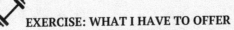 **EXERCISE: WHAT I HAVE TO OFFER**

Jot down a few things that make you an extra special human being. What can you offer someone that would make them the happiest person in the world? What makes you shine and stand out? Don't be shy or hold back, this is just for you!

Examples:

I know how to make homemade sushi!

I can always make someone laugh.

I always know how to brighten someone's day!

_____

_____

_____

_____

_____

_____

_____

_____

_____

_____

_____

_____

_____

_____

_____

What Is Love, Really?

Over the course of this book, I will share all the practices that got me from a place totally lacking in self-worth, to being totally confident in my intrinsic value as a woman. But first, let's dive into what this complicated word, *love*, really is.

Great thinkers and poets have been trying to encapsulate what love is for thousands of years. What's clear is that everyone wants and needs love. Animals want and need love too. Love seems to be something so mystifying, so elusive and enchanting that trying to express it often leaves us dumbfounded. "Yeah, why did I drive 13 hours unannounced to show up at that person's doorstep ready to tell them how I feel? Oh right...love." You see, love is like the law of gravity; you can't see it, taste it, smell it, or hear it, yet you know it exists, and it's pretty much going to win every time.

One night my husband and I were at a concert. We were dancing and vibing, staring into each other's eyes. It was overwhelmingly loud and completely silent all at the same time. Then it hit me like a tidal wave. Suddenly I came to the realization, and I understood with my entire being, that this thing we call "love" ***is the most powerful energy in existence!***

Let me repeat that again;

LOVE IS THE MOST POWERFUL ENERGY IN EXISTENCE!

How do I know this to be true? Well, think about it. Love moves across and through time and space without any boundaries. We can feel love for someone on the other side of the planet as if they are right beside us. We can feel love for someone who has long since passed away and is no longer in physical form. We can even have love for people and things we have never met! Now that's a trip. I even believe that *love has the magnetic power to draw two beings back to one another lifetime after lifetime*! And if you don't believe in past lives, that's OK, because love will still inexplicably pull you and your Cosmic Love Partner toward each other until one day you finally meet. Love connects us all by invisible strands that send and receive energy. What you put out, you receive back. Therefore, my motto is "The more love you give, the more you receive." More on this later in **Love Lesson 7, Appreciation**.

"Love" is such a big word that seems to encompass many different types of feelings. That is why the smart and clever Greeks had seven different words describing the various types of love.

Eros - Romantic love, it is passionate, and sexual.

Philia - Friendship, or companionship, sometimes born out of a romantic (Eros) love.

Storge (store-jay) - Familial love between parents and children.

Agape (a-ga-pay) - A spiritual type of love. Universal love, God love, altruistic love.

Ludus - This defines a more playful, less committed love. It's the art of flirtation and seduction.

Pragma - Similar to how it sounds, it's "practical" love, shared common goals, and *reason* describe this love.

Philautia - Self-love. This can take on healthy and unhealthy personas. Healthy self-love, which is what this book is about, is driven by building self-esteem and self-respect. Unhealthy self-love veers into the world of "hubris," an inflated sense of status, and arrogance, and narcissism.[1]

As you can see, love is multi-faceted and dynamic. Knowing the different types of love can help you define what it is you're feeling or experiencing. I believe all these facets of love, in their healthiest forms, are important to have in a cosmic love relationship. It's all the various facets of a diamond that make it sparkle in the light. Eros (passionate love), is immensely important, but overtime your burning hot bonfire may cool down and become hot sizzling coals for a while. If your relationship lacks Philia (friendship), or Pragma (practical love), and is only based on Eros, the relationship won't last. Look to cultivate love in a relationship that shines from many different angles.

> *"The giving of love is an education in itself."*
> Eleanor Roosevelt

---

[1] For more information about these seven types of love see: https://www.psychologytoday.com/us/blog/hide-and-seek/201606/these-are-the-7-types-love

"For he who would proceed aright in this manner should begin in youth to visit beautiful forms; and first, if he be guided by his instructor aright, to love one such form only - out of that he should create fair thoughts; and soon he will of himself perceive that the beauty of one form is akin to the beauty of another, and that beauty in every form is one and the same."
Plato

The first time I read this quote, I was so struck by it because it perfectly encapsulated my own journey with love. In my teen years, I was shrouded by darkness in the form of pain from injuries, anorexia, bulimia, a discordant relationship with my alcoholic mom, a suicidal best friend, a less than ideal living situation, and a disingenuous coach. I was filled with anger and not a lot of hope. Until one day, I gave myself an opportunity to find something I did like or love about my life. In that moment it was the view from my room which looked out into the verdant forest. Fluffy Grey Squirrels were chasing each other, Blue Jays were flying through the tree branches, and thick fog was rolling in, making the pine needles drip with glistening dew. A profound appreciation and admiration for the beauty of nature re-emerged from the depths of my being, and I felt renewed.

In that moment a thought came to me - I decided that I didn't believe in Heaven or Hell; that we experience the best and the worst of things in life, and that, in and of itself, is Heaven and Hell. This realization and awakening opened a doorway to love in my life. Nature captured my heart, and over time that love grew. I see how this snowball effect of love started with something as simple as the view from my room, and grew into Cosmic Love from there. When Plato suggests to "create fair," or beautiful "thoughts," and that this will cause one to "perceive that beauty of one form is akin to the beauty of another," I take this to mean that we can cultivate the bloom of a love large enough to reach the cosmos, out of the seed of loving one small thing.

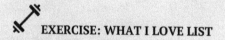

EXERCISE: WHAT I LOVE LIST

What is something you easily love? For me it's nature and animals. Maybe for you it's babies, or great works of art, the ocean, the stars, or the moon. Whatever it is, you can literally start with the love you have for that one thing and allow it to open your heart up to more and more love until you are so full of love that it just flows out of you abundantly and unrestricted.

Write down whatever you love or makes you feel love in your heart and describe what you love about it.

_____

_____

_____

_____

_____

_____

_____

_____

_____

Who Are You, Really?

You are the infinite in temporarily finite form.
You are a spiritual being having a human experience.
You are a limitless being with infinite love to give and receive.
Do you see the trend?

Think of the vastness of the universe. The size and magnitude of it is practically incomprehensible. The energy or frequency of love has absolutely no boundaries between time and space, and it can reach and occupy the entire expanse of the cosmos.

You, as a single individual, have the ability to capture that boundless energy of love, allow it to course through you, become you, and then share it with everything you encounter. You can share it with a beautiful flower you see while out on a walk. You can share it with your dog or cat, or turtle, or bird, any animal or creature you meet. You can share it with the trees, the air, the water, the food on your plate, the person in front of you, your parents, siblings, on and on. When you finally recognize that you contain this expansive capacity to love, and you share it openly and generously, your life will instantly open the doors for you to receive this love in return. This doesn't mean that your CLP will appear instantly, but rather, the starting point for them to appear manifests in the instant you share your love with others.

The universe is Love. Therefore, it is constantly supporting us to come back to love, but we need the wisdom to recognize this.

Sometimes, and unfortunately, the lessons show up as an abusive partner, sometimes they show up as disease or illness, even as the loss of a loved one. Everything that happens to us, or that comes into our lives, is the universe presenting us with an opportunity to love ourselves more. The saying goes that you can't truly love another until you love yourself. If that is so, then we must find ways to deepen our self-love. The simplest act of hugging ourselves is a great action to take. We can even kiss ourselves! When you were a child and you hurt yourself, what did your parent or caretaker do? They probably kissed it better. We can continue to offer ourselves this same love and care even when we get hurt as adults. Gratitude, compassion, and saying 'thank you' to our bodies, to our lives, to our environments (everything that surrounds us) - these are all great steps to take toward deepening love for yourself.

For example, since no one taught me how to love and honor myself, it took having multiple people do the opposite (use and abuse me), for me to wake up to realizing that I don't want to be treated like that anymore. The same can be said for a recurring ankle injury I had for many years. Every time my ankle would cry out in pain, I would get angry at it. I treated it like a bad stepchild who was ruining my life. I was constantly (both consciously and subconsciously) sending energy of resentment and rejection to my "bad" ankle. Then one day I realized that every time my ankle was hurting, it was just calling out for love. I began to see my ankle as a hurt little sensitive baby that needed my love, attention, and care. I started massaging my ankle and sending it so much gratitude and love for all the incredible things it's enabled me to do and for all the agony it's been through. The pain in my ankle was gone the day after I had this realization. It still comes back now and then, but now I know how to heal it from the inside out, with love.

The power of love is as infinite as the space it occupies. It's when we get caught up in our small-minded egos that we forget this and things in life appear contracted, limited, darker even. Love is light, and light is love. The more love we cultivate within ourselves, the more light we can radiate out into the world. And the more light we radiate, the more darkness we dispel. So, while you may have been drawn to this book to help yourself manifest the best relationship, by doing this work you are helping raise the frequency of love on our planet. In essence then, every living thing on earth benefits from your love.

"Light is to darkness what love is to fear; in the presence of one, the other disappears. All the darkness in my life—the fears, neuroses, dysfunctions, and diseases—are not so much things as the absence of things. They represent not the presence of a problem but rather the absence of the answer. And the answer is love. All fearful manifestations disappear in the presence of love."
Marianne Williamson,
A Year of Miracles: Daily Devotions and Reflections

How Does This Work?

"I was in darkness, but I took three steps and found myself in paradise. The first step was a good thought, the second, a good word, and the third, a good deed."
Friedrich Nietzsche

The universe is governed by certain laws. One of those laws is *The Law of Cause and Effect*. A *cause* is anything you think, say, or do. When you make a cause, the effect is immediately dispersed into the universe. You will meet the effect at any time that is appropriate according to your karma. If you consciously make positive causes, you are creating positive effects. And vice versa, negative causes create negative effects. Your causes also create your karma. The good news about this law is that it means you have the ability to change your karma.

From this moment forward, try to really pay attention to the thoughts you are thinking, the words you are saying, and the actions you are taking. All of these will have profound effects on the types of relationships you will attract into your life. Are you quietly thinking to yourself at times, "All the good ones are taken" or, "I'll never find someone to love me" or, "I always attract partners who won't commit"? These small and seemingly inconsequential thoughts create ripple effects of energy and vibrations that communicate with the universe. What you put out there, you receive back. This is why it is imperative you change your narrative.

Like attracts like. It is strict, but it's true. Personally, I find it freeing to remember this. It forces us to rise up out of victim mentality and blaming. It demands that we look inward for how *we* can change, how we can co-create and shape our destiny, as opposed to waiting for our circumstances to change and looking outward expecting others to change first.

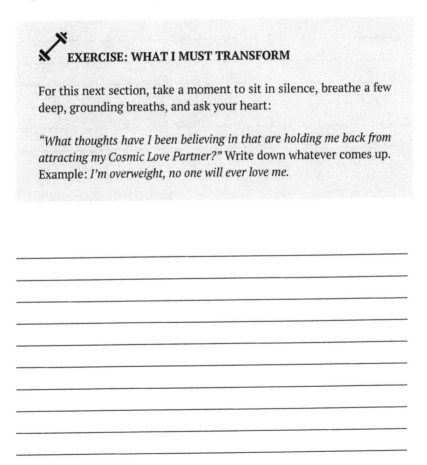

EXERCISE: WHAT I MUST TRANSFORM

For this next section, take a moment to sit in silence, breathe a few deep, grounding breaths, and ask your heart:

"What thoughts have I been believing in that are holding me back from attracting my Cosmic Love Partner?" Write down whatever comes up. Example: *I'm overweight, no one will ever love me.*

_____

_____

_____

_____

_____

_____

_____

_____

_____

_____

Now ask your heart: "Based on previous relationships, what are the challenges or patterns that I want to change and shift?" Write down whatever comes up. Example: I want to change my fear of speaking up.

_____

_____

_____

_____

_____

_____

Next, heartstorm on ways that you can change in order to make a cause toward seeing these aspects of your life change. What causes can you take to transform those previous patterns? Example: Learn how to communicate my needs more clearly.

_____

_____

_____

_____

_____

_____

_____

I want to plant a seed in your field of dreams. As you do the work to call in your CLP, ask the universe for a partner who, when the two of you come together, make a positive contribution to the world. In other words, a "world peace partner."

Around the time I began my Buddhist practice and made my list, a petite older Japanese woman named Yuki took me under her wing and nurtured me in my practice, and with delicious home cooked Japanese food. Mmm! She would say to me with strict but compassionate direction, *"Chant for your "kosen-rufu" partner!"* My what?! Kosen-rufu is a Japanese phrase that can translate to "world peace." Because I trusted her, I followed her guidance and began chanting and directing my intentions toward meeting my kosen-rufu partner, even before I really understood what that meant. Now with retrospect, I see why she guided me in this way. A world peace partner amplifies your power for good. A world peace partner is going to help you become the best version of yourself. A world peace partner is a teammate in the game of life, and ultimately shares the same values as you. So, harness the opportunity through your intentions, journaling, prayers and actions to manifest a partner that can work alongside you in creating a better, more peaceful and loving world.

"Love does not consist of gazing at each other,
but in looking outward together in the same direction."
Antoine de Saint-Exupéry

Choosing Love

One night I was trying to fall asleep, a good state to receive messages in, and it dawned on me just how impactful it is on our lives when we make causes rooted in love. When we think, speak, and act from a place of love and with a love filled heart, we create so much fortune for our lives. It's difficult to encapsulate the profundity of this into words.

I have witnessed the effects of living like this in my own life, and it leaves me in a state of awe. This is why I'm writing this book. I want to share the miraculous benefits of love with you! I want you to experience spontaneous joy, unbridled abundance, blissful relationships, beauty around every corner, vibrant health, supreme faith, wholehearted happiness, life in technicolor, and mystical support from the universe. Love is free, it's available to everyone no matter who you are; it's unlimited, and in fact, it fuels itself. The more love we create within us, the more love there will be moving and affecting the workings of the world.

Everything in existence has a counterpart and an opposite. Think of positive numbers and negative numbers; batteries have positive and negative currents; there's life and death. Yin and Yang represents the natural rhythm of life and is present in everything.

The counterpart to love, is fear. These two opposing forces are at war with each other, and in case you couldn't already tell by the state of the world, fear is currently winning. The planet needs love more than ever. We have an opportunity to create a wave of love warriors, or warrioresses, if you prefer. I call us warriors because it takes courage to love, and to choose love. It is a choice after all. In any given moment, we are offered a choice with how we are going to react to someone or some-thing, how we are going to respond, how we are going to take action and treat ourselves or treat others. Fear is devious. Fear, like love, also fuels itself.

Fear is oftentimes easier, and more comfortable to give into. It flows downhill, which if you've ever let yourself run down a hill, you know that you effortlessly pick up steam as you go. Love usually pushes and stretches us. It's an uphill climb. Taking those first few steps might feel challenging, but like with any muscle, the more you work it, the easier it gets. And I promise, the views from the top of Mount Love are exquisite and worth all the effort!

I may make it sound easy to just be loving all the time and then life will be great. The truth of the matter is that we are human; we have all the emotions, all the sufferings, all the feelings within us that are vying for their moment to shine. So of course, there will be moments you dip, moments you don't act or react with love, and that is OK. In Buddhism there is a saying, "ho-nim-myo" that means "From this moment forth." When we make a less than loving cause, we can reflect, apologize when necessary, reset, and then redetermine to do better next time.

I want to challenge you to choose love every chance you get. "Choose love" is like a mantra that I use to remind myself when I feel that pesky fear or negativity creep in. It has helped me immensely when heated moments arise between loved ones. It has helped me when I feel afraid of speaking up. It has helped me in times when I feel stuck and don't know how to move forward.

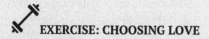

EXERCISE: CHOOSING LOVE

From this moment forward, look for ways to implement the mantra, "Choose love." Take note of how it transforms your actions, and the effects it produces. When we "choose love," we send ripple effects of love out into the world, into the universe, and those ripple effects touch everyone and everything.

Never underestimate the power you possess and produce from choosing love!

Increasing Your Self-Worth

Everyone wants to know how to gain self-worth. Where does self-worth come from? Will it just come to me someday? Wouldn't that be nice. The media will have you believing that self-worth comes from looking a certain way, eating a certain way, living a certain way, and having certain things. The noise can be deafening in my opinion. The single best way I have found to cultivate self-worth has been through *self-reflection*. Self-reflection is one of our greatest tools. Just like how you use a mirror to see how your outfit looks or apply your makeup, it's as important and necessary to find ways to reflect on what is in your mind and heart as well.

To do this, I recommend meditation of any kind, as well as reading books on self-improvement, journaling, spending quality time with animals, and spending time in nature. These activities allow you to slow down, become more present, and get to know yourself better. In this fast-paced world of instant gratification, constant media consumption, and a go-go-go, do-do-do mindset, it is so important to carve out time to be with yourself. Get to know the true you.

Who are you? What do you like? Who do you want to be?

Take a moment to reflect on these questions now. This section will hopefully evolve as you do. Write a little something now and come back to it over time. Self-inquiry is an ever-evolving process. I am still uncovering the answers to, "Who am I?"

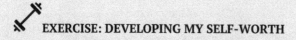

EXERCISE: DEVELOPING MY SELF-WORTH

Write out what makes you truly happy. What are some favorite child-hood memories? I mention childhood because this was when we were closest to our purest selves. You can also write down some affirma-tions of how you want to feel, and what you are envisioning for your future self. If your wisest, most inspiring version of yourself ap-peared in front of you, how would you describe them? Answer in the form of, "I am..."

_____

_____

_____

_____

_____

_____

_____

_____

_____

_____

_____

_____

_____

_____

"Self-reflection is the school of wisdom"
Baltasar Gracian

Making self-reflection a practice, will change your life forever, for the better. Through self-reflection you will cultivate self-awareness, and this is how you fundamentally change your karma. When you change and sparkle from the inside, your environment will change and sparkle back. This will result in attracting better partners, seeing more beauty in everything around you (including yourself), experiencing a deeper sense of meaning and happiness, and feeling as though you are in rhythm with your highest vibrations.

As your self-worth blossoms, so will your confidence. Confidence is proven to be one of the leading traits of attractiveness. It communicates to the other person that you know who you are, you're comfortable in your own skin, and you are just fine with or without the other person which releases any air of neediness. When you are confident, people are drawn to you. Confidence produces the energy of optimism, hope, and poise. We will explore confidence in the next section.

Increasing Your Confidence

One of my favorite ways to boost my confidence is by trying something new. Chances are you're better at this new thing than you think, and at the very least, you will walk away with a new skill in your back pocket. And who knows, maybe a new-found hobby or passion. That is how I got into Muay Thai kick-boxing. I took a class, loved it, and got hooked. Two years later I found myself in a boxing ring fighting in Las Vegas! You could try taking a painting class, learn how to blow glass, how about singing lessons? If you're tight on extraneous funds, find groups or meet ups that do fun activities together like hiking, photography safaris, language groups, etc. There is no shortage of free workshops online these days. Free Zoom gatherings, classes and workshops are happening all over the place.

Another way to build confidence is through physical exercise. Not only will your pumped-up endorphins boost your mood immediately, but you will feel better about your body too. I highly recommend martial arts classes like Muay Thai, Boxing, Kick-boxing, Hapkido, Krav Maga, Kali, Tai Qi, Judo, Taekwondo, Karate, etc. The years that I was deeply into Muay Thai kickboxing, my confidence soared as my strength and toughness grew. I felt like a badass punching and kicking on the daily. Looking back at that time in my life, Muay Thai came to me as I was healing from the unhealthy relationship with my coach, and as I was coming to terms with the end of my competitive figure skating career. It toughened me mentally and physically, and it gave me a healthy outlet to funnel my anger and rage. I really cannot advocate self-defense classes for women enough! Being confident that you can defend yourself, if necessary, helps give you a dose of added sexy swagger. ***KAPOW!***

One day I was cleaning out my desk and I came across a collection of cards that I had kept over the years from friends and family. I decided to read them all and see if I was ready to let any go since they were piling up. I was blown away by what a joyful boost of confidence it gave me to read old forgotten messages of love, encouragement, and friendship. If you have old cards stashed somewhere, make a point to go through them and see how those loving messages infuse you with a warm hug of confidence!

Since I'm on the subject of reading messages of love and encouragement, another effective method of increasing confidence is, *affirmations*. Affirmations are like mantras that you repeat over and over to yourself until what you're affirming about yourself becomes manifest. In my teen years before I started a Buddhist practice, I would practice affirmations daily. I had a board with a list of positive intentions toward how I wanted to feel about myself, or things I wanted to manifest in my life. I even used them on the ice while I was skating to help put me in the zone.

Some affirmation examples:
"I am strong, beautiful, fit, healthy, wealthy, and happy."
"I love myself more and more each day."
"My physical body, my mental body, and my spiritual body are all in alignment with my highest vibration."
"I am walking, talking, living, breathing encouragement to the world around me."

Once I started my Buddhist practice, I fused these affirmations with the active meditation of chanting out loud, *Nam-myoho-renge-kyo*, thereby increasing the power of the vibrations of the words I was saying. How this works is that everything is vibration. Words have vibration or frequency. The word "gratitude" is a high vibration, whereas the word "jealousy" is a low vibration. The mantra *Nam-myoho-renge-kyo* resonates with the frequency of enlightenment or Buddhahood. Fusing my affirmations (mental intentions), with the physical vibration of chanting, I believe, exponentially increases their power and effectiveness.

For more information about chanting, you can visit: www.SGI-USA.org or check out www.Buddhability.org

Maybe you've heard, but affirmations can get a bad rap. The superficial interpretation of affirmations reduces it down to such malarkey as, "Just repeat to yourself, "I am amazing and I am manifesting a million dollars" and ta-da, all your problems will disappear!" On a deeper level though, affirmations are incantations. They are vibrations fused with intention, spoken into the ether, like a prayer or a spell. When done so with humility, grace, purpose, connection to spirit, AND taking action, that is when the universe conspires to support you and direct you toward your visions.

Let's take some action.

EXERCISE: DEVELOPING MY SELF-CONFIDENCE

Write down some exciting ideas on how you can increase your self-confidence or self-worth, and then start tackling that list. Feel free to also include things you already do that make you feel good about yourself. You can include affirmations here too.

Take that CrossFit (or yoga) class I've wanted to go to.
Set a timer for 10 minutes every day to meditate on my affirmations and future visions.
Ask the next guy I'm really attracted to for his number.
Give a compliment to someone I don't know every day when possible.
I am always mindful of holding doors open for others.
I'm good at asking questions and listening.

_____
_____
_____
_____
_____
_____
_____
_____
_____
_____
_____
_____

*"With realization of one's own potential and self-confidence in
one's ability, one can build a better world."*
His Holiness the Dalai Lama

_____
_____
_____
_____
_____
_____
_____
_____
_____
_____

Increasing Your Life Condition

Thank you. These two simple words are powerful and magical invocations! I'll tell you why. Saying, or rather, invoking, "Thank you" opens us up to receiving the invisible gifts life is always offering us. "Thank you" not only brings us more to be thankful for, but it also immediately alchemizes any perceived negative situation into something that creates value.

How to implement this sorcery:

Let's say you get a cold. You have to miss work, you have to cancel plans you made with friends, you feel yucky, have no energy, your throat hurts, and you are just plain bummed, maybe even mad. Take a moment of quiet stillness and acknowledge all those feelings. They are OK to have and are certainly OK to feel. After you have felt them, say, "thank you" to your cold. Continue to sit in your quiet stillness and see if a message arises as to what the cold is offering you. Maybe it's time to rest. Maybe it's answering one of your prayers to have more downtime, or to work less, or to have a reason to binge watch a new show that you previously had no time to get into. Whatever it is, I guarantee you there is a message of healing there for you.

This practice can be applied to any situation. One of my mantras is, *"How can I get to a place where 'thank you' is my response to everything that happens to me?"* You can develop this muscle by invoking "thank you" to everything good as well.

A ladybug landed on you, "Thank you!"

The garbage collector came and picked up your trash, "Thank you!"

The trees and flowers in your neighborhood are healthy and blooming, "Thank you!"

A flock of geese just flew overhead, "Thank you!"

You can afford and enjoy a delicious and nutritious meal, "Thank you!"

Literally anything and everything we experience gives us a reason to be thankful. With consistent practice of responding, "Thank you" to life, your vision and your perception will change into being able to see the gifts on offer all around you, at all times!

This is a great time to listen to my Abundance Mediation at: www.sierramercier.com/meditations

Volunteering and being of service is another great way to increase your life condition. There is an abundance of ways you can give back to your local community, or anywhere for that matter. Andre and I created and produced a travel series online called, *Love Set Run* that shows you how to consciously volunteer in abroad. You don't have to leave the country to volunteer though. Check out a local animal shelter, or a food bank, or do your own beach or park cleanup. Giving back can be as simple as picking up trash if you see some where it doesn't belong or offering something to someone in need.

STEP 4

FINDING CLARITY

"Until you are clear nothing will be.
The moment you are clear everything will be."
Rasheed Ogunlaru

STEP 4: Finding Clarity

Now that you are armed with your specific list of important qualities, and you are taking steps along the path to deeper self-worth and radiant confidence, let's dive into **clarity**:
"The quality of being certain or definite."
"The quality of transparency or purity."

Getting clear on the inside is just as important as the outside. This clarity I'm talking about refers to clearing the mind, body, and spirit. I believe it's important to become an open and clear vessel so that you are ready to give and receive unlimited love.

In this next section, we will explore how to clarify these aspects of mind, body and spirit as it pertains to love. Though I break them down individually, in truth they are all related to each other. As you clear or purify each dimension, you will begin to bring your being into harmony. Think of your beingness as an instrument. When it's in harmony, the tune you emanate is balanced and melodic. When your beingness is stagnate in a particular area, or unclear, the tune it produces is erratic and incoherent.

The law of *like attracting like* is quite unforgiving, therefore it is vital to bring our lives into a harmonious vibration so that we can attract a partner who is vibrating harmoniously with us.

Clarity For The Mind

Exes, almost all of us have them. They have loved us, left us, hurt us, and really messed us up. They can feel like a heavy weight, they can even feel like they still have power over us, or quite possibly we are still not over them. In my case, just before I met my husband, I was the "collector" type. Even if a relationship didn't work out, I'd always keep them (exes) as friends and as somewhat of an open door, like a "what if," or a "maybe it could work out someday." I really just don't like goodbyes.

Shortly, and I mean just two weeks after I met Andre, I was encouraged by an intuitive friend to close all the other doors (metaphorically speaking). *"But wait! I just met this guy and you're telling me to cut ties with all these other people, some I have known for years?!"*

That was my initial reaction. Honestly, it was tough and scary for me to say goodbye and close those doors. I felt like I was going out on a limb with the possibility of falling and losing everything. In the end, I decided I was just going to ride the wave of trust and faith. I did it. I messaged the people who I had left doors open with, and said something along the lines of, "Thank you for being a part of my life. I have found someone that I'm very serious about being with. I wish you all the best, goodbye." You don't even need to have found someone yet to do this type of exercise, and you can be much more eloquent than I was. But, if you are ready for a real, long term, committed relationship, experiment with either writing letters to exes, or visualizing letting past relationships go. You can visualize cutting a cord between the two of you or imagining someone as a balloon that you let go of. *(Please don't release actual balloons as it is very harmful for the environment!)*

I know, there is always one that is especially hard to let go of. The one that got away. Your one and only true love... who broke your heart and never spoke to you again, right? Or who keeps coming around in mysterious ways making it difficult to let go and move on.

Take a deep breath... good... it's all going to be OK, I promise. I had one of these too. Losing him felt like losing my brother, my best friend. It gutted me from the inside out. It felt like someone ripped my heart out of my chest, threw it on the ground, and then proceeded to jump on it. Ouch! As my practice of everything I have talked about in this book continued, my heart grew stronger and more resilient. Deep inner wisdom began unearthing itself until I had a very simple yet profound realization; if this person who made me feel as great as he did is *not* 'the one,' then 'the one' must make me feel like a _____! You fill in the blank: "A million bucks!" "A freaking Goddess!" "A limitless, amazing, shining star!" Once I had this epiphany, the pressure of that heartbreak dissipated. I truly felt free, unstoppable, and excited for who I was going to meet in the future.

The universe works in mysterious ways and has quite a sense of humor. When we make changes in our lives, often we get tested right away. For me, as soon as I closed those doors, a friend called me and professed his love to me. He said that I was the only one that made him happy. He asked me to leave Andre, come live with him, and if we were still happy after a month together, he would put a ring on my finger. It was an emotional conversation, but I held my own and told him I wanted to be with Andre. He responded that we couldn't be friends anymore, which, for a "collector type", is the kiss of death. I knew there was no coincidence in the timing of this, and that the universe was testing me to see which door I would walk through - doubt or faith. I chose faith, and the rest is history.

While we are on the topic of exes, once you find your dream partner, guess what? They are probably going to have exes too. Sometimes this can bring up jealous and vindictive thoughts. Since this is a journey of self-transformation and love, let me tell you right now, there is no room, and no need for jealousy in a cosmic love relationship.

After Andre and I met, and started dating in a serious way, one of his formers popped up and tried to muddy the waters we were in. Initially this left a sour taste in my mouth, and I could sense that she was trying to make sure I knew he was "her's" first. But then I decided I wanted to get to know her better. It turned out that she and I had quite a few things in common. This realization gave me a whole new perspective on exes. If your partner dated someone before you, chances are you and that other person have some things in common. You might even really get along. So don't be too quick to defend your castle by shooting arrows. Be open and curious to the question, "How might we be similar?"

After you have identified some things you may have in common with your partner's exes, you might feel a kindredness or connection to them. Choose to see this other person with appreciation. Didn't you have people come into your life showing you what you want or don't want in a partner? Well, your partner's exes were the same great teachers for them, ultimately leading them to you. Be grateful, compassionate, and loving. This doesn't mean you have to be friends. It's just an opportunity to transform any negative emotions into more light and love.

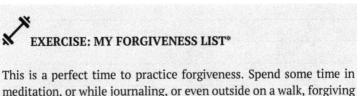

EXERCISE: MY FORGIVENESS LIST*

This is a perfect time to practice forgiveness. Spend some time in meditation, or while journaling, or even outside on a walk, forgiving people from your past for any and all things they may have done that hurt you. Especially take time forgiving yourself too. Forgiveness helps us move beyond our past into a new, brighter, lighter future.

Use this space to write out anything, or anyone that needs your forgiveness.

*Refer back to this list when you get to the section for my Forgiveness Ceremony in Step 5, Love Lesson 1.

_____

_____

_____

_____

_____

_____

"To err is human, to forgive, divine."
Alexander Pope, An Essay On Criticism

Clarity For The Body

Now let's get your body tuned up and ready for cosmic love!

Pay attention to the foods you're eating. *What does the food I eat have to do with finding true love?* Everything is made up of energy. When we eat food, we are absorbing energy from whatever we ate. To get your body vibrations up and in a more loving place, I recommend eating as cleanly as possible. This means avoiding or limiting fast foods, processed foods (pre-packaged foods), excess refined sugars, fried food, excessive alcohol, GMOs, and especially factory farmed meats.

I am not here to tell you to ascribe to any kind of eating lifestyle, but I will share a little bit about my own journey with nutrition. For eight years and throughout my competitive skating career I was a vegetarian, and I was dairy free for nine years. I dabbled in veganism, and pescatarianism too. In my mid-twenties, I was encouraged by a health practitioner to start eating meat again. Despite my moral reluctance, this change in my diet had very positive effects on my physical health. What I have come to learn and realize is that it's not about prescribing to a particular label, unless that truly works for you, but rather it's about tuning in to what feels right for your body and *eating consciously with intention.* Nowadays, I try and follow my intuition. (Emphasis on the "try.") Some days I'm drawn to a lot of green veggies, other days I'm attracted to orange foods like butternut squash and carrots. When I eat animal protein, I honor the animal by vowing to use their life force to make a positive impact in the world. It never hurts to experiment with trying different things and seeing how your body feels. Just remember, every body is different, so what works for one person, may not work for you, and vice versa. Yet there is no denying that eating a clean, well-balanced diet will make you feel better, think better, act better, and do better. All causes for creating more loving effects. This doesn't mean you can't enjoy yourself now and then and have a piece of cake, or a glass of wine or two. This is about living your best life, and that might mean treating yourself every once in a while.

It's your awareness and intention behind everything you do that matters most! So, the next time you have a meal, take a moment to think about the food in front of you. If there is meat on your plate, recognize and honor that a heartbeat of a living, breathing creature was part of that. If you have a beautiful salad, think about all the seeds that were planted to grow those veggies, the people and resources that nurtured and grew them, the farmers that harvested them, and all those who played a part to get them from the ground, to a grocery store, and onto your plate.

My Buddhist practice is all about changing karma. I believe that when I feel the need for animal protein in my body, I have a responsibility of changing that animal's karma by utilizing their life force to contribute to the world in a positive, value creating way. Find ways that resonate with you on how you can transform the food that fuels you into an intention that radiates love, and that honors the interconnectedness of life. Whether you are vegan or not, all kinds of living organisms contribute to growing, sustaining, and nourishing our lives. Having reverence for this profound interconnection creates harmony in our bodies, and that creates harmony in the world.

Movement

Moving your body, in whichever ways you can, is an act of self-love. I am not suggesting you become a gym rat or a body-builder, unless that makes you feel good. What I am suggesting is that carving out time dedicated to moving your body, stretching your body, exerting your body will create waves of benefits that go beyond the obvious.

The obvious is the health benefits of keeping our bones strong, and muscles toned, as well as the mental health boost exercise produces. Less obvious is the way in which vigorous movement of the body literally shakes free stagnant energy and emotions no longer serving us.

I am a huge advocate of dancing. Dancing feels so good and it can even be done in the privacy of your own home. My husband and I like to host dance parties at our place, even if it's just the two of us. Throw some of your favorite tunes on, add some party lights for added effect, and let loose!

Somatic release is another movement practice with deeply profound benefits to help clear your body. Somatic therapy gets you out of your intellect and into any stored emotions like anger, sadness, rage, fear, etc. and helps you to release these often repressed energies. This type of therapeutic work goes beyond the scope of talk therapy and truly helps you release any subconscious buildup of emotions stored in the body. This type of work has helped me immensely!

Sex

While we are on the subject of the body, let's take a moment to talk about sex. The fact of the matter is that biologically for women, sex typically binds us, whereas for men, it can be as inconsequential as a workout at the gym. In Steve Harvey's book, which I recommend by the way, "Act Like A Lady, Think Like A Man," he says to wait 90 days before sleeping with a man.

Personally, I don't believe it needs to be so calculated like reaching a goal end-date, but the point is that if you are really into someone, and especially if you know that you tend to attach more after having sex, then just wait. If the person you are into or dating is on board with taking things slowly, then that is a sign they respect you and are into you.

The more embodied you become by doing the steps within this workbook, the easier it will be to stick with your personal principles. Men will typically always want to have sex with you and will try whatever tactics they can think of to get it. Ladies, giving in to a persistent man when it comes to sexual encounters will not make him like you more. Take the risk of him not liking you for not giving it up and save yourself for a more worthy and deserving partner.

Enjoy the sexual tension and build up. Let the flirtation and seduction last as long as it possibly can because once that line is crossed, you can't get it back again. If you do end up dating, or even marrying this person, you will have plenty of time to explore each other sexually.

Clarity For The Spirit

This chapter is dedicated to the importance of finding a way to connect with the greatness of the universe. Or in other words, connecting to the greatness of YOU!

You are a microcosm of the macrocosm!

You are an entire universe unto yourself!

The next time you are out and around a large group of people, imagine that each person is their own universe. Even your dog or cat is their own little universe. This silly little exercise gives us a wider perspective of reality and helps us connect to the greater pulse of our universal selves.

I have already mentioned chanting, meditation, praying, and spending time in nature as ways of connecting to your spirit-self, but there are other ways to access the realm of spirit as well. Physical exertion, being creative, painting, playing an instrument, dancing, being with animals, cooking (alchemy), exploring plant medicine, even volunteering with a local charity organization (being of service) are ways to connect our earthly-selves with our spirit-selves. Each of us have been given unique gifts and callings and these are expressions of spirit in physical form. For me, it's figure skating. If my soul could express itself, it's by dancing across a frozen canvas.

We touch this infinite part of ourselves when we are completely present. When we become totally present, we can feel life's true eternal nature. Let's give it a try. Go ahead and while you're reading this, just start becoming aware of your breath, the rising and falling of your lungs within your chest. Feel the air travel through your nose and then downward as it fills your lungs. See if you can notice and feel the edges of your lungs pressing against your rib cage with each inhalation. Just be here with this awareness for a few moments. Close your eyes if it helps you focus on this feeling. If an unrelated thought pops up, just notice it, let it go, and come back to the sensation of your breathing.

When I'm in this space, I like to imagine someone or something on the other side of the planet breathing with me. When Andre and I volunteered at a lion sanctuary in South Africa, I watched as the steam rose from a lion's exhale one cool winter morning. I keep this memory with me and will picture a lion breathing at the same time as me. I imagine their chest rising and falling, and I think about how we are breathing the same universal air. This immediately connects me to the vast, yet intimate and interconnected nature of life on our extraordinary planet. Stay with your breathing buddy for a few moments, and then bring your awareness to the fact that every living creature on the planet is breathing right now. This rising and falling of breath is evident in the waves, in the plants and trees, the winds blowing. Beings are taking their last breath, and beings are taking their first. We are all connected through this simple act of breathing. The very pulse of life waxes and wanes in us all. This rhythm connects all life since the beginning of existence. This is the eternal reality of life and the infinite aspect of the universe existing within you.

The universe, source energy, God, Great Spirit, whatever you choose to call it, is always ready to support you in having more love, because the universe *is* love. The energy of love is swirling around us at all times, available to us whenever we want it. When you follow these steps I have laid out for creating clarity of the mind and body, clarity of the spirit will begin to come quite naturally because all these aspects are connected and work in harmony with each other, supporting one another.

Our spirit is clear when we are seeing life through the lens of love. When our spirit is clear, we are more intuitive, more magnetic, and we are able to manifest more readily; we see synchronicities, and we are quite naturally happier. Our life force is expanded. We feel supported by the unseen forces of the universe. We trust our lives! No matter what challenges and experiences come our way, when we are aligned with a clear spirit, and have profound trust in our lives, we can face challenges in life head on and transform them into sources of benefit.

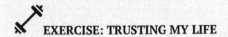 **EXERCISE: TRUSTING MY LIFE**

"I trust my life" is an affirmation or a mantra I regularly employ, especially in times of uncertainty. Experiment with feeling into the vibration of, "I trust my life." What does it mean for you to trust your life? Jot down a few things that spring to mind.

_____

_____

_____

_____

_____

_____

_____

_____

_____

_____

_____

_____

_____

_____

*"All I have seen teaches me to
trust the creator for all I have not seen."*
Ralph Waldo Emerson

Your Environment

When I say the word environment you probably picture the trees outside and nature, but when I'm talking about "your environment," I mean *everything your eyes fall upon at any given moment.* That is your environment.

If you haven't yet, please take eight minutes to follow along with my meditation on how to transform your environment into abundance at **www.sierramercier.com/meditations**

"Esho funi" is the Japanese concept for the oneness of life and its environment. Your environment is quite literally a reflection of yourself. "As within, so without," said Hermes. This is another very strict law. I suppose a law by virtue must be strict. It means that we must take full responsibility for whatever is in our lives, whether it serves us or it hurts us. There is profound freedom in understanding this principle.

If we can take a moment to step back from ourselves and just observe what is in our environment, be it abundance (or lack thereof), health or illness, joy or despair, it is in your life because on some level you have created that. Now before you close this book and throw it at me, or someone you don't like because you're thinking, "It's not my fault my ex was a narcissistic a**hole!" I just want you to ponder for a moment, "What is it about 'me' that attracted this kind of person into my life?" It doesn't have to be an ex, it can be a friend in your life. Just meditate on it. It might take days or weeks, or a psychedelic journey for an answer to reveal itself, but reflecting on our environment in this way allows us to change our karma and it prevents us from attracting the same challenging lessons over and over again. Trust me, it's worth examining. This is how we grow and evolve consciously.

"Whenever you are about to find fault with someone, ask yourself the following question: What fault of mine most nearly resembles the one I am about to criticize?"
Marcus Aurelius, Meditations

I'll give you a personal example. I had a friend in my life who I always seemed to have some issues with. We loved each other, but always had to "work" on our friendship. It was like we were a couple who needed couple's therapy just to navigate our friendship. I decided to look at her as a mirror of myself and examine what it was that I didn't like about her. One thing that arose was her constant need for validation. I accepted that I had a constant need for validation too. This new awareness of myself allowed me to go about transforming my own need for validation and become a more self-confident version of myself.

Who in your environment is reflecting something you don't like, and how can you change yourself in response? Just ponder.

Maybe it's not a person, but a circumstance in your environment that you wish to change. Do you struggle to create financial abundance? I have struggled with this too. Through my own self-reflection I discovered that lacking belief in my value as an artist has made it difficult for me to earn money as an artist. Where my work lies is in changing any small-minded beliefs about myself and taking actions toward claiming my worthiness as an artist with great value to offer the world. This is a process I'm currently working on, and this book in your hands is part of that journey. Thank you for being here with me!

Challenges and struggles that arise in our lives are often a result of our small-minded, negative beliefs. This goes for relationships of all kinds: romantic, platonic, familial, and cultural. Doing the work to transform our narrow minded and negative beliefs into optimistic, hopeful, loving, altruistic beliefs, is what will create the greatest results in our environment. Changing our environment begins with changing ourselves first from the inside out.

So, you might be thinking by now, what does all of this have to do with finding true love? Like I shared earlier, I used to attract men that didn't value me, who took advantage of me, or who just didn't want anything real and long term. I could choose to look at those experiences as a victim, pointing my finger and saying, "Men are a**holes." But instead, I consciously chose to view those experiences as a reflection of my own inner landscape. This self-inquiry revealed a pretty big disbelief in the value of my life, because if I truly valued myself, would I have let these men treat me the way they did? Absolutely not.

Another thing I wish to illuminate for you, is that as your perspective changes, your world changes. Let's say you are where I was, and you keep attracting jerks into your life. Does this mean you're a jerk? No, of course not. It's not that easy, or literal. But ask yourself, what makes that person a jerk? Is it because they don't respect your time? Honestly ask yourself, "Do

I respect my time?" Chances are you may find that you have failed to set firm boundaries around when you are available, and instead you let the other person dictate when they see you, causing you to sacrifice your needs to please theirs.

Here is where perspective is everything: You have identified where in your life you have played a role in attracting this type of person into your environment. The next step is to see that person as a teacher sent mystically into your life to teach you something. If you allow this person to teach you something about yourself, rest assured you will be free of jerks in no time! I can't really guarantee you won't ever date another jerk, wish I could, but I can guarantee that each time you encounter someone that disrespects you in some way, as long as you view that person as having a mission to teach you something, you will grow, transform, and you will be that much closer to finding your CLP.

Lessons I have learned from some of my "teachers" have been: how to really value myself as a woman, how to respect and honor my time, how to not be afraid of being honest about what I want, and what to pass on to my daughter so she can (hopefully) avoid making the same mistakes I made.

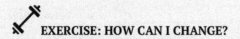 **EXERCISE: HOW CAN I CHANGE?**

Use the following space to reflect and write down recurring themes in the people you tend to date or attract. Then do some journaling around what that might be reflecting back to you. List anything in your environment that doesn't feel supportive, or that you know you want to change.

_____

_____

_____

_____

_____

_____

_____

"Nothing ever goes away until
it has taught us what we need to know."
Pema Chodron

_____

_____

_____

_____

_____

_____

_____

_____

STEP 5
THE LOVE LESSONS

"Wherever you are, and whatever you do, be in love."
Rumi

STEP 5: The Love Lessons

My love lessons are quick and easy tidbits of wisdom to support you along your mission to finding and keeping true love going strong. They are lessons and truths that have sustained and guided me in my relationship, as well as others.

(If you like video content, you can find a web series of most of these lessons at: https://lovetv.co/author/sierramercier/)

Feel free to bounce around. This section does not need to be absorbed in order. Go where your spirit moves you!

Most of all, have fun with these. I find that sometimes we can get so serious when it comes to self-transformation and personal development, but we really can't forget to enjoy ourselves along the journey.

I had a vision once when I was meditating on success. The image that came to me was that of a dog chasing a carrot. The dog had the happiest, slobberiest grin on its face as it chased this moving carrot, and the message I received was, "The dog is going to catch the carrot, but that's not the point. The point is how much fun the dog is having chasing the carrot." So please, have fun expanding your life! Delight in digging deeper into your soul, connecting with your heart, and sharing what you find with the world around you.

1. Love Yourself

"Those that go searching for love only make manifest their own lovelessness, and the loveless never find love, only the loving find love, and they never have to seek for it."
D. H. Lawrence

Become a love magnet! Psychologists say that to really love others, we first must love ourselves. Self-love has many layers to it, and I'm sorry to break it to you, but likely you will be working on those layers your entire life. Hooray! By layers I mean the many forms that self-love manifests in.

We must approach self-love from a whole-body perspective. If you are just getting started on your self-love quest, I recommend starting with your **diet**. Oops, did I say a bad word? These bodies we inhabit for hopefully a full century are our temples. A temple is a sacred place. If you love traveling like I do, chances are you have visited a temple at some point. These holy housings are carefully guarded, immaculately maintained, and are meant to help bring you closer to spirit. Our own bodies that we have been given to walk through this enchanted, magical exhibition of life are the most unique and exquisite temples on earth. One in eight billion and counting! Choosing good quality nutrients to feed our bodies with is an excellent way to begin and maintain a self-love journey.

Exercise is another offering we can make to our earth vessels that has unbelievable benefits. Aside from keeping us looking strong and healthy, exercise has proven mental health benefits, and can even help us release stagnant emotions. So, start moving and grooving!

Media, whether it is the news or your social media feed, it's all a form of energy that we absorb and take in, and this affects us too. Honestly speaking, when was the last time you scrolled through Instagram and 30 minutes or an hour later you say, "Wow, I feel so much better!" #NEVER! Social media especially is causing us to look outside ourselves more than ever. We are seeking acceptance, love, validation, answers, how to eat, how to dress, how to think, how to look, all outside ourselves. When really all the answers we could ever possibly need for our own life, are right there already within our very own heart. The more time and energy we spend looking outward, the further and further away we are pulled from what is true to ourselves. Give yourself some major love and take a break from the doom scrolling, the constantly negative news, and anything that doesn't make you feel **better** and **lighter**.

How you *feel* is the key. When we are really honest with ourselves in acknowledging how someone or something makes us feel, and we allow our highly intelligent and perceptive bodies to guide us, we will naturally make better, more holistic, healthy choices.

The layers I just talked about are physical. Other layers of self-love are more cerebral, like self-acceptance, and forgiveness.

Accepting ourselves just as we are, is a major act of self-love. I like to view accepting myself as a vow I make to my highest self, because keeping a vow, like a promise, makes it something I can continue to come back to as a reminder when I veer off course.

"I vow to unconditionally love and accept myself just as I am."

Forgiveness is right up there with *acceptance*. We have all done things in our lives that we are ashamed of, that were possibly harmful to ourselves and/or to others. Holding on to shame, allowing it in any form to rule over us, is like pouring salt in our own wounds. Forgiveness lightens our load to carry. It frees us from self-inflicted perfectionism. It is yet another way to show yourself some love.

Let's take a moment here and perform another ceremony.

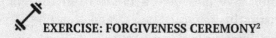 **EXERCISE: FORGIVENESS CEREMONY**[2]

I learned this ceremony at a healing retreat center in Peru. I was encouraged to write down everything I have ever done that I could think of that I wanted forgiveness for. Things I have done to myself, and to others. Just a big, long list of, "I forgive myself for _____."

---

[2] Refer to the list you made in Step 4, (page 79) for this exercise.

It was a very emotional exercise tapping back into these shameful, hurtful memories. It forced me to really look at myself honestly and examine where I misstepped, where I harmed myself, and where I harmed others. When I was done with my list, the piece of paper that held all my forgiveness felt like it weighed a ton, a literal ton - it was so heavy. It contained so much energy I didn't even realize I had been carrying around all these years. I took this double-sided sheet of forgiveness history, hauled it to the fire pit, and sat heavily by the fire as I re-read aloud to myself everything I had written down. When I was through, and felt ready, I tossed the list into the flames. In a mere instant it vanished into weightless ash. It was truly remarkable how this piece of paper that I had poured my heart into, and that felt so dense to me, vaporized before my eyes in a single moment. It was such a relief! It was absolutely beautiful.

Fortunately, you don't need to go to Peru to do this kind of ceremony. All you need is paper, something to write with, some nice alone time, and a fireplace, or fire pit. I do recommend that you always keep a bucket of water nearby when doing anything with fire. I do not recommend doing this ceremony inside if you can avoid it.

Please set aside the space and time to perform your Forgiveness Ceremony before continuing.

"The weak can never forgive.
Forgiveness is the attribute of the strong."
Mahatma Gandhi

Ah, take a deep breath. Do you feel lighter now?

As you continue to practice turning your love inward, I also encourage you to start turning your love outward - but don't go running for that dating app just yet, missy! Start by just stepping outside and taking a walk around the block. What do you see? Do you see a tree with beautiful, gnarled roots, a thick, sturdy trunk, green or colorful leaves? Maybe the tree has flowers on it, or fruit! Maybe birds are finding refuge in the tree. Admire this being before you. Hug it even! I love hugging trees. They are such humble, earnest beings, and master meditators. Find something to love about the tree; maybe it's the artsy, abstract shapes the bark creates. Maybe you notice a conga line of ants dancing up the tree. Maybe you find love for the color of the leaves contrasted against a sapphire sky. Once you become aware of your appreciation and love for the tree, say thank you, and move on to something else.

Perhaps next you will come across a flower. Take note of what you can love and appreciate about this radiant explosion of color and intricacy. Notice the divine symmetry of the petals. Or the perfect imperfectness of it too. According to a healer I know, flowers are the highest vibrational beings on our planet. Time to befriend some flowers!

> *"Flowers are the music of the ground,*
> *from earth's lips spoken without sound."*
> Edwin Curran

Is someone approaching with a dog? How can you love and appreciate that furry, happy being? What about another person walking past you? Oh, they might have really beautiful hair. Tell them! "Your hair is beautiful!" It feels great receiving compliments and it feels even better giving them out. It's like handing out flowers to people passing by.

Make it a daily practice to give genuine compliments whenever possible. I always keep my eye out for a way to praise someone. I gift them the compliment, and then allow the mystic workings of the universe to perform its magic. Since I do this often, I find that I receive more compliments from strangers, I attract kind-hearted people to cross paths with, and I have made serendipitous connections - just to name a few wonders from the simple act of giving out compliments. And believe it or not, these are all acts of SELF-LOVE.

Where you can earn mega karma bucks is when you tell another woman how beautiful she is. I don't know why, but it's challenging, and it sometimes feels awkward to tell another woman how beautiful she is. There is so much unnecessary competition between women. We are all beautiful in our own unique ways. Making it a practice of shining light and love on other women has been truly transformational for me. How I do it is if the thought crosses my mind, "Oh wow she's really beautiful." I find a way to tell her, if possible. Not a single woman has ever been offended or weirded out by this. If you're a man reading this book, the same thing goes for you. Muster the courage to tell a woman, or another man, how beautiful or handsome they are; a "Looking good man." will do. It's like depositing treasure into a karma savings account every time you do this.

Another way of cultivating more love is to think of your love like the sun's rays. The sun shines its radiant warmth out into the galaxy in all directions whether a planet is there to reflect it back or not. When we become like the sun with our energy of love emanating out, it doesn't matter who or what you encounter, your warmth will be felt, and it will nourish. This is a great intention you can set at the beginning of the day. Determine to be the sun everywhere you go, and with anyone you meet. Some people may not return your light, and that's alright, just keep on shining! Like my Yogi Tea wisdom says, "Plant kindness and gather love."

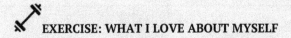

EXERCISE: WHAT I LOVE ABOUT MYSELF

This is a great place to bookmark. I learned this exercise from a very wise healer. On the following pages, list 20 things you love about yourself. This might be more challenging than you expect. If that is so, congratulations, you're human! I'm not usually this strict, but for this exercise you do have to find 20 things. No skimping or cutting corners. I know you can do it!

Once you have your list, read it aloud to yourself every day. For how long? I don't know, you be the judge. You can do it for a week straight and see how you feel. You can try the 21 day habit forming method. You can use it like a multivitamin and take a dose each morning. But just give it a shot. Here are some samples from my own list: I love my sense of humor. I love my big heart. I love my self-discipline. I love my good health. I love my eyes. I love my strong legs. I love my love of nature. I love my innate wisdom. You get the idea... Your turn!

1. I love my _____

2. I love my _____

3. I love my _____

4. I love my _____

5. I love my _____

6. I love my _____

7. I love my _____

8. I love my _____

9. I love my _____

10. I love my _____

11. I love my _____

12. I love my _____

13. I love my _____

14. I love my _____

15. I love my _____

16. I love my _____

17. I love my _____

18. I love my _____

19. I love my _____

20. I love my _____

"You yourself, as much as anybody in the entire universe, deserve your love and affection."
Buddha

2. When You Know, You Know

Q: How do I know if someone is "the one?"
A: We have all heard this saying before when someone describes finding "the one." Well, that's because it's true! There really is this deep calm sense of knowing that I describe as two souls recognizing their mate in one another, hence a soulmate. The term soulmate has a wide array of definitions and beliefs behind it. I encourage you to explore them all and see what resonates for you.

I believe we have multiple soulmates. A soulmate is someone you made an agreement with in a past life to help one another evolve in this life. That agreement can be between you and a cat, a dog, even an octopus. Hey, don't laugh, go see "My Octopus Teacher" on streaming right now! What this means is that soulmates can come into our lives, but it also means they can leave once the contract is fulfilled. Since we are spiritual beings having a physical experience, the physical experience of that soulmate leaving can be devastating. However, don't dwell in sorrow, you have more than one soulmate.

Another term often described as being even more consequential than a soulmate is a "twin-flame." The idea behind this comes to us from the Greeks. It is thought that our soul split into two halves and in each lifetime, our mission is to reunite with our other half. This reunion doesn't happen every lifetime. Since our mission in each lifetime is to evolve consciously and spiritually, there will be lifetimes where that work must be done on our own, or with other soulmates, before we can be ready to reunite with our twin-flame. There are many differing opinions on the twin-flame relationship, but what I believe is that once both halves have achieved the appropriate soul evolution, then the twin-flames will meet to merge back into one.

I will refrain from trying to describe what a twin-flame relationship is like because truthfully, I think it depends on where each person is on their own consciousness evolution journey. My twin-flame relationship is going to look different than yours simply due to the nature that we are different people. I feel it is better for us to define the meaning of these things for ourselves. Cause and effect and karma make for each person's experience of love and relationship to be completely unique.

Ok, so how do I find my twin-flame? My advice for you is to continually work on your own personal self-development. Continue to become the best, most shining version of yourself. Polish your inner life so brightly that your twin-flame won't be able to miss you. Imagine finding an unpolished diamond. If you don't know what to look for, it will just look like a basic rock. But if you have been polishing your life, that jewel within is going to be sparkling and brilliant. There will be no mistaking that's a diamond, not a rock. So rather than looking for your twin-flame outside yourself, work on looking for your own flame of greatness within. The brighter your flame glows, the more likely it will be that your twin-flame finds you.

Something else to keep in mind, is that "When You Know, You Know" does not mean it happens right away. Sometimes love takes time to cultivate and grow. You might start out as friends for several years, and then one day realize you want to be together. Trust the mystic timing in all things.

In my research of other couples who have experienced this "knowing," I have come to postulate that we leave little hints, little breadcrumbs to help us remember and find each other lifetime after lifetime. For me, it was Andre's tattoos. He finished a full sleeve of traditional Japanese block style tattoos on his right arm eight days before we met. He had a feeling that getting these tattoos would help him meet someone; not necessarily romantically, but just that they would bring people into his life. After we met and I got to know him, and his tattoos, I felt on a soul-coded level that in a past life, he told me he would mark his body so that I would know it was him.

One married couple I spoke with discovered they grew up five minutes away from each other, but they didn't actually meet until after college. I consider these synchronicities clues and signs that we leave behind to help us remember each other, or to remind us that we are on the right path. So be on the lookout for these kinds of hidden messages and synchronicities between you and your soulmates and/or your twin-flame.

3. Friends First

Q: I think I'm in the friend zone, is that bad?
A: Don't be afraid to seek out friendships. When getting to know someone in the early stages of dating, really reflect on if this person is someone who you would want to be friends with. Do you feel like you can really open up to them, tell them anything? Share about your past? Even your deepest, darkest secrets? Not that you need to rush into that, but just consider it. Could you fart in front of them? I'm serious. Again, I don't mean right away, but being able to just be a human being in front of someone else is a form of intimacy.

All jokes and human bodily functions aside, **Friends First** is something I absolutely, hands down believe is essential in a Cosmic Love Partner relationship. The truth is, if you are going to spend the rest of your life with this one person, you are going to be spending A LOT of time with them, and who better to spend your time with than your best friend?! It's not even worth your time seeking out a relationship with someone whom you don't feel is, or could be, one of your *best* friends.

A best friend is someone who believes in you, who lifts you up when you are down, who is there through thick and thin. These are qualities to both cultivate and to look for in a partner. If you are dating someone and they don't treat you like your best friend would treat you, then it might be time to move on. And the same goes for how you are treating them. Like the Golden Rule says, "Treat others the way you want to be treated."

Andre and I built our entire relationship on the foundation of friendship. We became friends first; I knew he would be there for me as a friend no matter what. Then when we took that leap into a romantic relationship, it felt secure and like our friendship just got better. When you begin to build a new relationship, work on building a friendship first. Even if you know right away that the physical attraction is there, take your time, seek friendship with this person, and then once that is established, it will make the next step of your relationship that much stronger and more exciting to explore.

4. Don't Play Games

Q: I heard I'm not supposed to text for three days after meeting, otherwise he will think I'm too eager, is that true?
A: Games are for the field, or on a board, NOT for relationships. Look, you are trying to attract true, cosmic love here, right? You don't want to waste any more time, right? You're a mature, responsible adult, RIGHT? Well, stop with playing games and just be real, **please**!

I used to be the "go with the flow" type. I would start seeing someone, start to like them, but play it cool and tell myself to just, "go with the flow." The problem with this approach is that I wasn't being totally honest with myself. Underneath this play it cool attitude I was really hoping the guy would like me enough to ask me to be his girlfriend and want a relationship with me. Then when the person I was dating would or would not get what they wanted, they usually bailed. I was left feeling used or rejected. Can you relate? Then one day a friend told me about Steve Harvey's book, "Act Like A Lady, Think Like A Man" and my approach was changed forever. In this book, Steve encourages women to say what they want. He explains that men will get away with whatever they can, so when a woman comes along who is smart and self-confident enough to know, and SAY OUT LOUD what she wants, he either has to man up and give the woman what she wants, or walk the other way.

I decided to give this strategy a shot the next time I *really* liked someone. The very first time that Andre kissed me, I told him right then and there that I was at a point in my life where I wanted a relationship. If he wasn't looking for one, then we needed to stop kissing and I would be on my way. In all honesty, this really caught him off guard, but it opened the door for an important dialogue about where we were in our lives, and what we were both looking for. Eventually he grabbed me, kissed me really hard and said, "Yes!" "I want to make this [relationship] work."

The next time you are really into someone, (please do not do this on the first date), but as you get to know each other and while you are building a friendship, if there's electricity between you, say what you want. If the other person is repelled by this, then they're not the right person for you (at this time), and now look at all the pain and anguish you saved yourself from. Congratulations! Next. My other tip is that *this is about you*! It has nothing to do with the other person. Co-dependency would be you telling the other person that you are ready for a relationship *with them*. Yikes. Major turnoff. Confident-Badass-Mature-Woman-Goddess-Babe says, "I really like you, and before we continue to expend either of our precious energies, I just want you to know that I'm at a point in my life where I'm really ready and looking for a long-term committed relationship. If you're not there, that's OK, but we're going to have to stop seeing each other." Or something of the sort.

Do not be discouraged if you get turned down a few times from this tactic. Look at it as a way of weeding through the cubic zirconiums until you come across a real diamond.

A friend that I was coaching for a couple years throughout her dating life had many men back away after she told them what she wanted. This scared her and she was worried that it wasn't the right approach. I told her to continue to be upfront and honest about wanting a relationship and ultimately marriage. She eventually met a man online who was truly her soulmate. He was on the same page and had been looking and waiting for her every bit as much as she was him. They are now happily married with two baby boys.

This approach does take knowing what you want though. There are times when you might not know what you want. That is totally OK. If this is you, my suggestion is to focus on yourself, your career, your health, and your spiritual practice. If you don't have one, start cultivating one. Your spiritual practice doesn't have to involve religion, it can simply be journaling every morning. Without self-inquiry, and continuing to date around, you will likely attract partners who also don't know what they want, who won't commit, and relationships that won't go very far. Be with yourself and be still enough for the quiet whispers to emerge letting you know what your deepest heart's desires are. Maybe that will be more *you* time. Maybe that will be a long-term committed partnership. Whatever it is, it's worth discovering.

5. Being Yourself Is Being Authentic

Sounds simple enough - *just be yourself*, but the truth is, when we first meet people, and even as we get to know them, we all have the tendency to act in ways in which we think the other person will like. Deep down we are all people pleasers screaming, "PLEASE LIKE ME!" This pattern may be stronger in some of us than in others. *Cough, "myself." This people pleasing side, especially in women, causes us to put ourselves in an inferior position to the man. Thanks to thousands of years of repression of the divine feminine, it is now every woman's karma. We want so desperately to be approved of, liked by, and desired by men that we will bend in whichever way necessary to get that approval. We will put our needs and desires second and the man's needs and desires first. We are often pressured into sexual acts and will engage even if we are not 100% into them. We give away our power and let the man call the shots all because of a deep and karmic desire to be approved of and loved.

This behavior is called "Seeking love outside yourself." It is a futile road and will lead to heartbreak every time. Even if it works for a little while, how exhausting and depleting to continue. The ultimate goal is to first seek the love you desire from *within* yourself. Approve of yourself, like yourself, put your needs and desires first, love yourself!

I want to clarify something though. Often I see a woman trying to reverse this power dynamic by swinging too far in the opposite direction and becoming demanding or expecting that the man bends to her wills and wishes. Sass, ego and attitude are not the antidote. Nor does it communicate that you are a powerful Goddess. Quite the opposite in fact. Men still want to feel like men. Chivalry is not dead! If you follow the steps in this book, you will build real, authentic, grounded, divine-feminine power that the other person will not only feel, but they will also respect and respond to. This my dear, is much more of a turn-on.

When you begin to operate from this place, better matches in mates will be drawn to you, and they will naturally sense that you don't need their love or approval. Instead, their company will become a compliment to yours as opposed to a contrast.

When I first met Andre, it was under the condition of becoming roommates, so there was a part of me that instantly felt like I could just be myself. I didn't feel the need to only be seen with makeup on or wearing some cute outfit all the time, only sometimes. (Wink!) Although I had a little crush on him, I felt comfortable and friendly enough to really just be myself, PJ's and all. When sparks began to fly between us, I came to realize that he really liked *me*, just as I was. Not me pretending to be someone who I thought he wanted me to be. Our love and intimacy deepened because there was no pretense in the way.

Guaranteed, if you are working at trying to be someone other than who you really are, you will end up attracting the wrong people. Once again, like attracts like. *The Law of Attraction* is another law of the universe. So, who are you deep down? Are you a goofball, but you are trying to be more serious? Are you actually quite serious, but you have been trying to be the life of the party? Or maybe you are very sensitive, but you mask it with overcompensated assertiveness. The more we allow who we really are, deep down, authentically to show up and emerge, the more readily we will attract someone who can mirror back their authenticity. Being ourselves gives other people permission to be themselves, and what a relief that is!

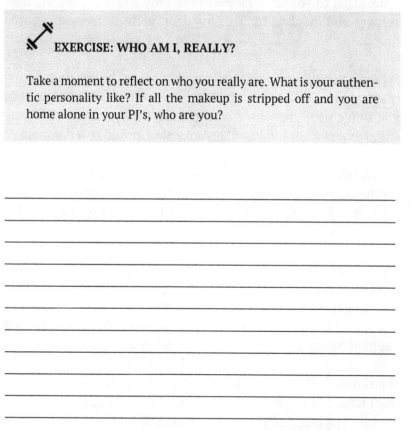

EXERCISE: WHO AM I, REALLY?

Take a moment to reflect on who you really are. What is your authentic personality like? If all the makeup is stripped off and you are home alone in your PJ's, who are you?

_____

_____

_____

_____

_____

_____

_____

_____

_____

_____

_____

_____

6. Honesty Is The Best Policy

"Honesty is the first chapter in the book of wisdom."
Thomas Jefferson

OK my friend, this is an important love lesson, so listen up! Well, yes, they are all important, but this one is especially important, because if ignored, it can get you into big trouble. Trust me, I learned the hard way.

Fibs, lies, half-truths, whatever they are, I like to think of them as weeds. In the beginning they just seem small and insignificant. "Ah, no one will notice. It's not hurting anyone so whatever!" But overtime those weeds begin to grow, and when they grow, their roots get bigger and sink deeper. Now your weed is a problem. It's taking up space, it's ugly, and poisonous. And guess what? When you go to pull that sucker out, it's going to be ten times harder than if you had pulled it out when it was just a little baby weed. Better yet, don't even let it become a weed in the first place. Displace it when it's a seed and tell the truth!

Here is an example:
Andre and I met, we fell in love, got engaged, and got married all within the span of about 14 months. Things happened *really* fast! But part of me still didn't feel like I had total closure with a past relationship. I was afraid to tell Andre about this in fear of him getting jealous or upset. Rather than being honest and

open about it, I kept it to myself and arranged to meet up secretly with this person in search of closure. We met up, it was awkward, certainly did not feel right, but at least I was able to get some of the closure I was seeking. This was my little weed.

Over time this weed would not stop bothering me internally. It kept poking me and popping up in random places and at random times. Eventually it was making me physically nauseous and sick. I knew the weed needed to be uprooted. I told Andre I had something to tell him that was very difficult. We went for a walk together and I explained what happened. It was such an enormous relief to have pulled the weed out. Fortunately, he took it well enough, and I was able to grow a lot from this experience. In retrospect, had I been open in the beginning and told Andre that I needed closure with this past relationship, he would have given me the opportunity to have the meeting without having to be secretive about it. The meeting would probably have gone better too. The whole painful experience made me vow never to keep anything from him again. Fast forward many years, our relationship is stronger than ever because we are totally honest with each other.

This type of honesty builds trust in a relationship. I can't even begin to tell you how good it feels to have absolute trust in your partner. Those of us who have been cheated on and have trust issues especially know the value of trust. Knowing Andre and I have 100% genuine trust in each other makes our relationship feel like we are floating in an ocean of warm Tahitian waters. It's comforting and healing, it feels safe, and I feel fully supported.

I truly don't want you to have to go through the pain and agony that I did in learning this lesson the hard way, so please heed my warning that no matter how uncomfortable or difficult something may be to talk about, honesty is *always* the best policy. Even if it feels scary in the moment, being honest will lead to dialogue and will help build even more trust and intimacy between you and your Cosmic Love Partner.

"To conceal anything from those to whom I am attached, is not in my nature. I can never close my lips where I have opened my heart."
Charles Dickens

7. Appreciation

"What you appreciate, appreciates."
Unknown

Welcome to one of my favorite tools. I call it a tool because I like to look at *Appreciation* as a tool we can keep in a toolbox. Just like when something breaks or needs repair we go straight to our toolbox for the pliers or hammer or wrench, the same can be true of appreciation in relationships.

This is an active application, meaning it requires conscious effort and can take some practice, but I promise you the effects are well worth it. Living in a state of appreciation has a myriad of benefits. It raises your life condition so that you can respond to situations in a more positive manner, it widens your empathetic embrace of others, and it colors and reframes negative experiences into advantageous ones. It's also contagious. When you start appreciating things and people more, your environment will reflect that appreciation, and appreciate!

The next time you find yourself in a squabble with a loved one (this is not limited to romantic relationships), and you start to feel that seething righteousness bubbling up wanting so badly to lash out declaring that you're right and the other person is wrong, take a breath and challenge yourself to think of something you appreciate about them. Do you appreciate that they always encourage you to follow your dreams? Do you appreciate that they share the household chores? Do you appreciate that you feel safe with them? Do you appreciate that they provide for you? Do you appreciate their intentions, their skills, their best qualities? Like I said, this can take practice, so don't wait until a quarrel happens to pull out the appreciation tool. I encourage active use of *Appreciation* whenever possible.

This is not, however, about putting on blinders and overlooking abusive behavior. If you are in an unhealthy relationship and being mistreated in any way, physically, verbally, mentally, sexually, this is not a time to use *Appreciation*. In a scenario like this, please call for help and get yourself out of that situation immediately and safely!

- Domestic Abuse Hotline: 800.799.SAFE (7233)
- Emotional Abuse Hotline: Text HOME to 741741

In an otherwise healthy relationship, when little arguments pop up where it doesn't really matter who is right or wrong, make the cause to take the high road. Just one thought of *Appreciation* will melt the tension. Don't forget to take a deep, calming breath, and then witness as your quibbles quickly dissolve.

Practice appreciating yourself too. What can you pat yourself on the back for? What makes you hold your head high and think, "Gee, I am a wonderful human!" When we lack appreciation for ourselves, it's even easier to lack it for others.

There are times when I feel like I really want to be appreciated for the things I do, like the laundry, or the dishes, or taking such great care of our daughter on a daily basis. When I'm feeling this need to be appreciated, first I pause and with a little pat on my shoulder or a self-hug say, "Thanks for doing the laundry, Sierra!" Then I find a moment to say to Andre, "I'm really feeling like I could use some appreciation for _____." This type of practice helps build a conscious, communicative, healthy relationship.

EXERCISE: MY APPRECIATION LIST

List all the things you appreciate about yourself.
Then list what you appreciate about your mom, and/or your dad, and your significant other if you have one.
Extra credit if you make a list for someone who really pushes your buttons. (Seriously, this is big!)

When you make your list, try to connect a memory with each thing you wrote down. For example, if you wrote down that you really appreciate how hard working your partner is - think back to a time when you witnessed their hard work in action and how it made you feel. This will imprint and highlight in your life the best aspects of those around you.

_____

_____

_____

_____

_____

_____

_____

_____

_____

_____

_____

_____

_____

_____

_____

_____

*"The deepest principle in human nature is
the craving to be appreciated."*
William James

_____

_____

_____

_____

_____

_____

_____

_____

_____

_____

_____

_____

_____

_____

_____

_____

_____

_____

_____

_____

_____

_____

_____

Caution:
The opposite of "what you appreciate, appreciates" is also true. The more time you spend seeing all the things your partner or loved one is doing to fall short, or is not good enough at, that is what you will see everywhere, all the time. This leads to complaint and complaining erases fortune. This is not about denying our shortcomings or those of others. Weaknesses are still important to reflect on and address. Rather, this Love Lesson is about deepening your recognition of the value of each individual in your life. The goal is to get to a state of life like this:

"It would be great if we could live cheerfully, enjoying life to the extent that we regard our partner's nagging as a sign of his or her good health and proof that he or she is still alive and kicking. When we develop a broad state of life, then even our partner's ranting and raving will sound like the sweet song of a bird."
Daisaku Ikeda

8. Your True Power

Humanity has for thousands of years divided the sexes in a way that puts men above women. Women have been subjugated, rejected, burned alive, raped and repressed for so long that I believe it has created a karmic blockage making it very challenging to understand how truly powerful we as women are. I look around at all the violence and destruction taking place on our planet and believe that it is a direct effect of the suppression of the divine feminine.

The power of women is akin to the power of Earth. Women, like Earth, are life creating, life giving, life nourishing. When we begin to see ourselves as powerful creators with unlimited love to give, and truly start to recognize our deep inherent value, then not only will we become more effective in our lives and in our communities, but we will attract better mates that value us in return. We will also give other women the courage to believe in themselves too. We have the power to create a wave of harmony restoring balance to the yin and yang of Earth and the universe.

Recognizing this power within you illuminates your inherent worth. When your self-worth is illuminated, you make causes reflecting that Goddess nature within, and by now you should know that Goddess rooted causes, will produce Goddess rooted effects.

My goal with this workbook is to get you to a place where you feel proud of who you are. You understand with your life how immensely valuable you are. You honor and treasure the gift of getting to be a woman in this lifetime, a teacher of how to love. I shared at the very beginning of this book that when women stand up with a deep belief in the sacredness of their existence, this will cause men to change, and to value and respect us back.

So much of a long-term relationship is about showing the other person how we want to be treated. If you are clear in your values, you can gently and compassionately guide and teach your partner how to treat you. This is what constitutes a conscious relationship. Practicing this over time will help restore the balance of divine feminine and masculine. This creates destiny changing ripple effects for future generations, and for our planet as a whole. That is your true power!

Did you know that you are capable of having a "heartgasm?!" Much like an orgasm, a "heartgasm" is a euphoric surge of energy emanating from your heart chakra. I experienced this after a meditation where I imagined harnessing all the love in the universe with my hands, and then blasting it out into the field of existence. I saw it reaching and touching everything and everyone on our planet. I felt it penetrate the hearts of dolphins in the sea, I surrounded my parents in this ecstatic field of love, and I pictured it embracing Mother Earth. I gifted it to myself as well. The following morning marked my 15th year of Buddhist practice. I chanted *Nam-myoho-renge-kyo* reflecting on my life over the past 15 years, and I reflected on the meditation I did the night before. Epic proportions of gratitude swelled forth in my heart initiating this "heartgasm."

Much like with an orgasm, once you have experienced this sensation, you are more easily able to recreate it. I was able to give myself multiple "heartgasms" that day! Contrary to what you may be thinking, this is not a selfish act. I am confident that the pulsing energy of love during a "heartgasm" reverberates into the collective field. When you combine the love of the universe with pure gratitude, you can create a supernova effect of healing energy for self and others.

The true power of women never ceases to amaze me. The true power of love never ceases to amaze me either. When these two potent forces collide, alchemize, and work together, they create and produce limitless possibilities.

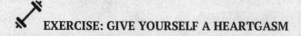

EXERCISE: GIVE YOURSELF A HEARTGASM

With your eyes closed, and palms open in a receptive position, picture love as an energy. You can give it color, or a pattern, or texture to help you envision the energy. See it occupy your surroundings and reaching all the way out through the cosmos. Now imagine drawing that energy into the palms of your hands. Doctor Strange style. You can even rub your hands together vigorously and then pull them apart slowly to feel the energy you have harnessed. Now turn your palms outward as if you're sending all that love into the collective field. Who do you see it touch? Let your imagination flow and visualize this limitless source of love permeating everything. Sustain this visualization and feeling as long as you can. Take. Your. Time. Finally, bring your hands to your heart and integrate all that love into your being as well. While in this space, conjure the frequency of gratitude by calling to mind and heart all the things you're grateful for. Take slow, deep breaths expanding your heart chakra and allow swells of whatever magic you created overtake you. Make an audible sound on your exhales to increase the sensation. Let tears flow if they come. And last, but not least, smile. Feel the warmth your smile brings, like the rising sun on a crisp morning. Luxuriate in this moment for as long as you can and know that you have the power to return here at any time.

9. Take. Your. Time.

As my South African friend, Amor, says, "You do you, boo." There is absolutely no need to rush into finding someone to be with. In fact, the more selective you are, I believe the happier you will be when you finally meet the *right* person. Taking your time allows you get to know yourself. What your dreams are, your passions, your likes and dislikes. What's important to you, what's not important. When we turn our focus inward and do the deep work to love ourselves, we will naturally radiate composure and confidence. Two very sexy traits.

Don't worry if your path looks different from everyone else's. Just because all your friends are married and having babies and you are still single, does not mean that something is wrong with you. Every moment of your life contains special gifts. In Buddhism there's a saying, "Dig beneath your feet, there you will find a spring." No matter where you are in your life, there is always something of value for you. Rather than looking outside yourself and comparing yourself to others, discover what this time alone has to offer you. Hey, it's giving you time to do this workbook! Maybe it's giving you time for a new hobby, or passion pursuit. Maybe travel and exploring is what you always wanted to do. Maybe you decide to train for that marathon you said you wanted to run. Listening to the messages your heart tells you, will open and reveal opportunities that you never could have had if you tried to be like your friends and be settled down at 25.

Not that there's anything wrong with being married at 25, because "when you know, you know" knows no age. I was 25 when I met Andre, and I turned 27 a week before we got married. But I had lived quite a full life for someone my age. I grew up as an athlete racing on the ski team, figure skating, and doing ballet. I left home at 16 to pursue a competitive figure skating career. I lived virtually on my own for over seven years all before I was 25 years old. When I retired skating competitively, I was devoted to martial arts and became a Muay Thai fighter. I taught figure skating lessons, I worked as a floral designer with my mom, I started taking acting classes, I apprenticed as a sushi chef. I really *lived* my life, so feeling ready for a long-term relationship at 25 felt right to me.

We are all on our own unique paths. Spend your time and energy doing what *empowers* you, makes you feel *worthy, valuable, beautiful, powerful.* **Live your life!** The right person for you will be inspired and attracted to you when you are doing the things that light you up.

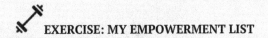

EXERCISE: MY EMPOWERMENT LIST

List whatever makes you feel emboldened and powerful!
Taking solo trips. Taking a new class. Writing poetry. etc.

_____

_____

_____

_____

_____

_____

_____

_____

_____

_____

_____

_____

_____

_____

_____

_____

_____

*"A mind that is stretched by a new experience can never go back
to its old dimensions."*
Oliver Wendell Holmes Jr.

10. Decide What You Want

"It is not in the stars to hold our destiny but in ourselves."
William Shakespeare

Decide - what kind of relationship do you want?

I clearly remember the moment I decided what kind of relationship I wanted. I didn't perform some special manifestation circle under the full moon or anything like that. Though of course you can if you want. It was just a quiet moment with myself. I may have even been driving, but I had the decisive thought that: I knew I was ready for a long-term, committed relationship, and if I were to marry the next person I dated, I was OK with that. That's it. It felt simple, it felt clean, and it felt freeing to know what I wanted, and then just let it be. Deciding or knowing what you want is so crucial because it empowers you. It's like having a map while you're traveling.

I see this happen to women a lot; they wait for the guy to decide if he wants the relationship to go somewhere.

What about **you**? What do you want?

If you want a relationship and you are with someone who can't commit, or get on the same page as you, then buh-bye! I know that may sound harsh, but time is our most valuable, precious resource. Why spend time spinning wheels that are not in alignment with what you want? If it's meant to be with that person, then truly nothing will stop it from being.

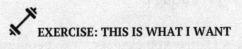

EXERCISE: THIS IS WHAT I WANT

Cue Spice Girls, Wannabe song:"I'll tell you what I want, what I really really want!" Take a moment to declare to the universe what type of relationship you feel ready for. Remember to be specific.

_____

_____

_____

_____

_____

_____

_____

_____

_____

_____

_____

_____

_____

_____

_____

11. Respect

True love demands respect. Have you ever seen two people argue? It's so painful. I grew up in an argumentative house. I have witnessed couples arguing with each other; strangers arguing with one another. I have even been the ugly arguer. What I believe it boils down to is a lack of respect. The dictionary definition of respect is: "due regard for the feelings, well wishes, rights, or traditions of others."

A Buddhist observation on the subject:

> *"Anger immediately creates a distance. When two people are angry at each other, their hearts are no longer close, their emotions are divided and they go miles apart. To cover that distance they yell. The angrier they are, the louder they shout. They are no longer in mode of love, of acceptance, of proximity. They are unable to hear each other, shouting is how they believe they can be heard."*

> *"And what happens when two people fall in love? They don't shout at each other but talk softly, they almost whisper, because their hearts are very close. There's little or no distance between them.*

When they love each other even more, they exchange even less words, more softly, they murmur, they whisper, yet they hear each other better, their bond strengthens, their love prospers. Finally, they may not even whisper, they only look at each other, silence becomes more potent than speech, that's how close two people can get when they are in love.

So when you argue do not say words that break your bond of love and make you distant from each other."

Though this parable is talking about anger, if respect were active here, the yelling would never have happened in the first place. In order to be loved at the caliber you deserve, first you must respect yourself, and second you must respect others. Everyone feels pain, sadness, joy, longing, loss, etc. When we recognize that fundamentally we are all the same, we can really start respecting one another, which will lead to much healthier and happier relationships.

12. Celebrate What You Wish To Create

One day I was standing in line at a Chipotle. Fancy, I know. There were two young women in front of me. They were both East Indian, and one of them was wearing a stack of bracelets that I knew meant she was recently married. I commented and congratulated her on her marriage. Her friend scoffed, rolled her eyes, and made a snide remark about all the attention she was getting and how "it's all about her." Clearly her friend was jealous. I felt sad that this happy young woman, in the joy of her celebration, had a friend that just couldn't be happy for her.

I'm sure we have all experienced something along these lines. That one friend that just can't be happy for you no matter what. To this I say, "Celebrate what you wish to create!"

When you see someone else scoring a new job, finding a soul-mate, or just living their best life, if that is something you want for yourself, celebrate it! Say, "Yes!" and visualize yourself in that position too. Send that person some love and congratulations. These actions communicate to the universe that you desire the same successes. It puts you in the same frequency of the things you want. It also strengthens your friendships when you can be genuinely happy for someone else's wins. In addition to all of that, it feels really good to live in joy for others.

When we see someone succeeding and it makes us feel fear, scarcity, lack, comparison, envy or jealousy, we are the one who suffers. Instead, use it as an opportunity to celebrate it as if it is your own success! Remember, anything we think, say or do has a consequence for our lives. Think, speak, and act on good intentions and your life is bound to be filled with things to celebrate.

"If you want to feel good,
you have to go out and do some good."
Oprah Winfrey

13. Gratitude

This superpower storehouse within you is a lifelong friend that will always be there waiting to fill your cup. Appreciation is the tool to employ when you are at odds with your partner or loved one. It's a tool for making yourself and others feel loved and recognized. But *Gratitude* is an inner journey. It's a bow of deep respect to the greatness of all things. When we lose gratitude, we lose ourselves. When we live in gratitude, our lives blossom.

What can you find gratitude for right now? How about the ability to read? Not everyone has that fortune. Gratitude journals can be lifelines; I've heard that Oprah keeps one daily. One of my gratitude "secret weapon" meditations is to go through every part of my body and express my gratitude for it. It goes something like this:[3]

- *I begin with my major body parts first: starting with my toes and feet, I offer gratitude for the way they get me around and help me balance. Then I'll move up to my legs, my knees, my thighs, my butt, my torso, my arms, hands, neck, and head - acknowledging each part for why my life is better because of it...*

---

[3] Listen to a recording of this guided meditation at: www.sierramercier.com/meditations

- *Then while I'm offering gratitude for my head, I think of my hair, my eyes, my ears, my nose, and my mouth and all of their virtuous functions.*
- *Next, I go inside my body and offer gratitude to my tongue, teeth, my brain, my throat/esophagus, my lungs, my heart, stomach, liver, gall bladder, spleen, appendix, pancreas, kidneys, bladder, intestines, colon, uterus, fallopian tubes, ovaries, cervix, vagina, yep I went there. (Modify as necessary.)*
- *Then I go even deeper into my body and send gratitude to my muscles, bones, tendons, veins, blood, cells, good bacteria, neutrons, protons, electrons, **everything I can anatomically think of** (without being an anatomy major) that makes my body function and operate the way that it does.*
- *Last but not least, the part that holds it all together, the largest organ of the human body, my skin.*

There was a period of time where I did this meditation at least once a week, and when I met up with a friend who I hadn't seen in a few months she exclaimed, "You are literally glowing!" I promise you that if you do this regularly, even just once a week, you too will start to glow from the inside out.

I really believe that when you are vibrating at your highest frequency, you are bound to attract the best possible partners. Not only that, but you will be feeling so good internally, loving yourself, that the chase for external love will die down. When you don't need someone else to validate you, you will stand out and shine. And who doesn't like shiny things?

In 2019 I was at a Buddhist retreat center for a multi-day conference. On the last day of the conference, I sat beside a lake on the property and chanted to this beautiful, surging fountain that gushes into the lake. I was mesmerized by the fountain's ceaseless outpouring. I was reflecting on a particular area of my life that I struggled with, but I was also reflecting back on the amazing weekend I had. I chanted with gratitude in my heart, and even gratitude for my struggles, and in that moment with the view of this bursting fountain, I decided I wanted to become a "fountain of gratitude" every day. I wanted to embody a never-ending flow and abundance of gratitude. I began chanting like this every day, that *"I am a fountain of gratitude!"* I saw first-hand the effects of my intention to be a fountain of gratitude bloom. I found myself experiencing so much grace and abundant reasons to be grateful.

Never underestimate the immense power of gratitude. Make a determination to become a fountain of gratitude in your own life. This will manifest as living in a constant state of awareness of all the blessings surrounding you. Washing your hands with soap - gratitude. Soaking in the nice view out your window - gratitude. Snuggles from a loving fur baby - gratitude. Having access to healthy, nutritious food - gratitude. I'm sure your list is endless, as is mine. Tune into it often.

14. Spiritual Partnerships

The paradigm is shifting. According to a mixed bag of astrologers, the *Age of Aquarius*, a time of harmony and coexistence, is nigh or possibly here. Traditional norms are breaking down and slowly being reconstructed into greater ideals. Women's rights are continuing to evolve. Humanity is awakening into a new level of consciousness, and you either get on board, or you get dragged, and having to get dragged is not going to be fun. What all of this means is that you don't want to just settle for a partner out of fear or resignation. If you have been called to this book, you don't want to settle at all, you are desiring to meet your *Cosmic Love Partner*.

What is a spiritual partnership?

Love in its greatest form helps us to become the best version of ourselves. It's not just meant to be a physical, an emotional, or an intellectual experience. Love is meant to be a spiritual experience. Despite the airy translucence of the word "spirit," spiritual partnerships in fact create the strongest of bonds. I highly recommend Gary Zukav's book, "The Seat of the Soul" for his take on spiritual partnerships.

To me, a spiritual relationship is one in which two souls decide, beyond the dimension of time in a past life or on another plane of existence, to help one another evolve into their highest selves. It is a soul level contract that also gifts each person the opportunity to experience the greatest teachings that love has to offer. In order to experience that though, choosing love over fear must be the foundation of the relationship. A spiritual partnership always presents opportunities to grow and expand together. Although some of that growing may be uncomfortable, there should always be a mutual and grounded understanding of, "We are in this together."

If you are in a relationship where the other person doesn't make you feel like they always have your back, or if they abuse you in any way, shape, or form, this is not a spiritual relationship. The last thing I want to see you do is stick it out with someone who doesn't meet you where you are, who doesn't wholly value the divine being you are, and who manipulates you with their false power and pretense.

Lastly, I want you to know and believe that someone out there is looking for you too! Trust that. Have faith and confidence that somebody is equally hoping and intending on meeting YOU, the person of their dreams. You can even begin to visualize this spiritual partner and yourself as two like-beings of light and love drawing closer and closer, being drawn to one another like magnets. Magnetize your CLP to you by working on being the one, to receive the one.

15. Don't Settle & Don't Give Up

The title says it all, so I guess my work here is done! Don't settle and don't give up!

If you're reading and doing this guidebook, then you feel a calling to attract the most fulfilling relationship. You have decided that this is important to you, and you are willing to do the work to manifest it. Bravo! I commend you because it is certainly not the easy route to take, but it is the most rewarding.

When I was in my early twenties, I made the lock screen on my phone a photo of a sticky note that said, "DON'T SETTLE." It was a constant reminder to myself of my value, of what I have to offer, of all the work I'd been doing, and of my commitment to honoring what I believed I deserved.

Choosing to not settle takes courage. It also takes patience, and it takes a ton of faith! If you are willing to devote yourself to the path of love, and I really hope you do because the world is in desperate need of more love, then you must become a warrior. Strong, dedicated, and fearless. Willing to risk love on the battlefield of life. The old adage, *"'Tis better to have loved and lost than never to have loved at all"* is really true. Love is a risk, but if it's something you want, you must take the leap.

This kind of love I'm talking about and guiding you toward is worth the work, worth the wait, and worth the risk. There is someone out there looking for you, meant for you. If you settle for someone simply because they have money, or because your family approves of them, then you are resigning the rest of your life to a sub-par experience. Rather than risking love, you are risking divorce, infidelity, loneliness, a whole host of challenges that arise when two people end up settling.

Just to be clear, I am not saying that it's wrong or bad to settle. There is no shame in settling. It's simply a choice. It's a *cause* that has *effects*. Not settling is also a *cause* that has *effects*. Which one are you willing to take the chance on?

Side note: If a relationship doesn't work out, that doesn't necessarily mean one or both of you settled. As mentioned earlier about soulmates and soul-contracts, perhaps a relationship ended because the intended soul-contract had been fulfilled. You will know if or when you are settling, because settling creates a very different experience.

And don't give up! A good friend of mine dated her share of duds and was becoming bitter, believing that maybe she just wasn't meant to find true love and that it didn't even exist. This friend was one of my bridesmaids and after our wedding she told me that seeing our marriage reignited her belief that true love really does exist. A couple years later she met her "one" and I was a bridesmaid in her wedding. The very act of believing that true love does in fact exist, is half the battle won.

> *"The journey from Kamakura to Kyoto takes twelve days. If you travel for eleven but stop with only one day remaining, how can you admire the moon over the capital?"*
> Nichiren Daishonin

16. Bonus: Love Vision Quest

It was the deep night of a full moon, and I was bathed in its electric illumination while being embraced by ancient rock formations in the desert of Joshua Tree. A group of us had come together for a vision quest. Each on our own unique journey, yet collectively providing the power of human oneness. I sat in meditation ready to give myself over to the deeper knowledge of the universe, open to the fusion of my own well of wisdom with the limitless wisdom of the cosmos.

I gave the quest a subject - love. "What is love?" What came to me was an image of a glowing pyramid, a holy and important temple, much like something you would see in Egypt. I entered this temple and inside was the rarest, most precious, valuable jewel in all of existence. It was enclosed in a case, illuminated by spotlights, and highly protected. This safeguarded jewel was my love.

This vision taught me how profoundly sacred our love is, and that when you decide to fall in love with someone, you are gifting them that hallowed, priceless jewel. This should not be taken lightly. Your jewel of love should be protected and kept safe until you meet someone that truly deserves to be given this jewel. Notice I didn't say guarded? Guarding your jewel of love means to withdraw it. Whereas protecting your jewel simply means to stand firm before it.

Each of you possesses a precious and powerful jewel of love. It lives within the temple of your heart. As you take the teachings I have shared with you in this book out into your daily life and into your future relationships, I hope that you find a vision of what your jewel of love might look like. Observe watching how it grows, acknowledging how much you value and prize it. Become aware of and attuned to how this jewel alters the way you perceive and respect your love. You, and your love, are infinitely valuable treasures. Display it, but protect it. Cherish it, and honor it. It is a reflection of your divinity.

"My bounty is as boundless as the sea,
My love as deep; the more I give to thee,
The more I have, for both are infinite."
William Shakespeare, Romeo and Juliet

Conclusion

"The only person you are destined to become
is the person you decide to be."
Ralph Waldo Emerson

Congratulations, you did it! Celebrate yourself for taking a leap into the unknown with me. Love is the greatest journey we can embark on. Love will forever be our greatest teacher and muse. Along this voyage you have bravely faced and identified your fears. You have surrendered to something bigger and are floating on the wings of faith. You have gained new perspectives and transformed poison into medicine. You are now a clear vessel ready to give and receive Cosmic Love.

Take a BIG, deep breath, throw your arms up in the air and release everything you have worked on to the universe with courage, hope, and of course... LOVE!

Feel free to use the following blank spaces to write out any notes, thoughts, reflections, and intentions you may have as you embark on your new Cosmic Love Partner journey.

_____
_____
_____
_____
_____

"Touched by An Angel"
By Maya Angelou

We, unaccustomed to courage
exiles from delight
live coiled in shells of loneliness
until love leaves its high holy temple
and comes into our sight
to liberate us into life.

Love arrives
and in its train come ecstasies
old memories of pleasure
ancient histories of pain.
Yet if we are bold,
love strikes away the chains of fear
from our souls.

We are weaned from our timidity
In the flush of love's light
we dare be brave
And suddenly we see
that love costs all we are
and will ever be.
Yet it is only love
which sets us free.

Actual Proof...

Sierra and her husband, Andre.

Their daughter, Reya.

About Springboard Edition

Would you like to make a difference, too?
Springboard Edition publishes the expertise of researchers and practitioners to make the world a life-supporting place.

Dear Sierra,

Since we first met on a Zoom call in one of my Masterclasses on Writing & Publishing, I knew I would support you in bringing your expertise to the world. Instantly, there was an understanding and trust between us, and I enjoyed our collaboration. Now that your book will touch the world, I wish you all the best with this project and beyond.

Ulrike (Uli) Posselt
Owner of Springboard Edition

From Experts. For the World.
Is your expertise life-supporting and relevant?
If so, let's have a chat: publish@springboardedition.com
https://springboardedition.com